# HELP, LORD!

A Guide to Public and Private Prayer

PAT McGEACHY

JOHN KNOX PRESS
ATLANTA

Unless otherwise noted the Scripture quotations in this publication are from the Revised Standard Version Bible, copyright 1946, 1952, and © 1971, 1973 by the Division of Christian Education, National Council of the Churches of Christ in the U.S.A. and used by permission.

Library of Congress Cataloging in Publication Data

McGeachy, Pat, 1929–
   Help, Lord! : a guide to public and private prayer.

   Bibliography:  p.
   1. Prayer.  2. Prayers.  I.  Title.
BV210.2.M3      248'.3     77–79592
ISBN 0–8042–2358–0

# CONTENTS

*for Sandy*

# I
# THE ART OF PRAYING

*Almighty God: you have no patience with solemn assemblies, or heaped-up prayers to be heard by men. Forgive those who have written prayers for congregations. Remind them that their foolish words will pass away, but that your word will last and be fulfilled, in Jesus Christ our Lord.*

A prayer for those who write prayers.
*The Worshipbook*
(Philadelphia: The Westminster Press, 1972), p. 202.

*If praying comes hard for you,* you may want to read this book straight through, for I have really had you in mind since I first knew I was going to write *Help, Lord!* Thank you for joining me!

But it is a mistake to think that you must read every book from front to back. *If you are a Bible-based person,* you may want to begin with the Old Testament section, or with the prayers of Jesus.

*If you're hoping to sharpen your skills at public praying,* you could even skip to the practical business in the back though that isn't the most exciting part.

Or, *if you aren't exactly sure where you are with regard to praying,* just jump in anywhere. This wasn't meant to be read at one sitting. Most of the thoughts are complete on each page. You might even want to try using the prayers for a couple of months at your daily devotions, though some of them are vastly more suitable than others.

However you come at it, you will soon discover that I am something of all four of the persons mentioned above and have been writing to myself in every case. I doubt if I have much to tell you that you don't already know. But I have done a whole crowd of thinking about prayers in the past forty-seven years, and it is demanding to burst forth. I would like to have you walk with me for a way, to start you thinking, to turn you loose, to make you mad, perhaps even excited about this ancient and modern art. Prayer *is* an art. It isn't usually one of the "fine" arts, like painting or sculpture, which are sometimes limited to the specially talented few, but a humble art, like that of conversation or folk singing. It belongs to us all.

I have a hard time distinguishing between the art of praying in public and that of private devotions. Of course I know there are differences. There are times when we must follow Jesus' orders to withdraw and pray in secret (Matt. 6:6), and there are other times when we need to gather in church for common worship, which was also our Lord's custom (Luke 4:16). In private prayer we don't worry much about grammar and phrasing; God knows the secret language of our hearts better than we ourselves. In public prayer, we may use the plural form of the pronouns, and be very conscious that we are praying with and for others. But it is important, even in private prayer, to express ourselves clearly (not so that God will understand, but so we will), and even in public prayer (perhaps especially there) it is important to be straightforward, honest, and natural.

So I am going to write about prayer as though its public and private practice were essentially the same. My method is to comment on a few prayers, a large number from the Bible, some from traditional liturgies, and a few from my own personal experience. I collect prayers. That is an unfortunate hobby, for prayers in that respect are like butterflies: if you collect* them, you kill them. Prayers were not meant to be dissected; they were intended to be lived. But there have to be lepidopterists and biologists, and by the same logic, I suppose, those who take prayers apart to see what makes them work. I sometimes wish I weren't in the business of teaching others about religion. Not that it's hard and dangerous work (Matt. 18:6); I knew that it was dangerous work when I started. But what I hadn't counted on was how difficult it is to be a person of faith yourself, when you are trying to pass it on to others. It's more fun to play football than to coach it.

In the rural community where I work there is great suspicion of prayers that are "written down." The implication is that this imprisons the Holy Spirit, and makes genuine prayer difficult, if not impossible. With this sentiment, I am in agreement. But I also think that most of us who pray "spontaneously," have an unconscious pattern "written down" inside. Test this yourself, by listening to the repetitions** of the informal prayers you hear. We will not escape from written prayers; they are either on paper or in our hearts. So the question is: what shall we write there? Let me push that athletics metaphor a little further, in the spirit of 1 Corinthians 9:25–27. I believe that developing the art of prayer consists in learning fundamentals (from the Bible, from the great prayers, and from a deepening understanding of life), until I become sufficiently well-disciplined to be free. An athlete will not do well at broken-field running until he knows the rules and the fundamentals quite well. In order to be given the earth as an inheritance, I must first submit meekly to training (Matt. 5:5). The Spirit will not be stopped, either by prayers printed in books, or on the printed circuits of the mind, provided they be put at his disposal. I remember overhearing someone criticize a "high-church" preacher because he "reads his prayers." To this, one of his parishioners, who knew and loved the old parson, bristled and replied, "He doesn't read those prayers! He *prays* them!"

Come, then! Let us pick away at a few prayers. The venerable ones will survive it; the lesser ones will deserve what they get. Pray that something happens to you and me in the process.

Pat McGeachy
Rockvale, Tennessee
1976

---

*It is true that there is a form of prayer known as a *collect*, but, according to the *Oxford Dictionary*, that means that the people were collected, not the prayers. A collect is a prayer to be used at a gathering of the faithful.
**Be sure to notice the word *petition* hiding there.

# II.
# SOME PRAYERS I HAVE OVERHEARD

*A prayer implies a promise as well as a request; at the highest level, prayer not only is supplication for strength and guidance but also becomes an affirmation of life and thus a reverent praise of God.*

Joey Adams quoting Walt Disney in *The God Bit* (N.Y.: Manor Books, 1975), p. 25.

*Lord, help me to see that trouble is only opportunity in work clothes.*

(From a church bulletin)

The first six words are a formula often used by those who write prayers to turn simple aphorisms into sentences that sound religious. Actually, this is not a prayer, it is an epigram. It would be far more honest to let it stand alone:

*Trouble is only opportunity in work clothes.*

By itself it is a fairly decent short saying, phrasing an old cliché in a fresh way, suitable for teaching purposes. But it is not addressed to God. In its context (the front cover of a church bulletin) it is addressed to a congregation. On that same bulletin, the formula is used to turn two other secular proverbs into prayers:

*Lord, help my words to be gracious and tender today,*
*for tomorrow I may have to eat them.*
*Lord, help me to resist the temptation to make a*
*mountain out of a molehill, simply by adding a little dirt.*

The question is not are these statements true, or wise, or clever, but are they intended to explain things to God, or to someone else? If (as I believe) they are really being used to teach a point to the people, whoever wrote them ought to have the honesty to let them stand as direct address, not disguise them as liturgy.

Whenever I hear a minister begin a prayer with the phrase, "Lord, help us to . . ." or "Lord, we know that . . ." I immediately become suspicious that he is praying *at* me, not *for* me. He has been given an opportunity afforded to few others in our society, namely a time to preach to us, instruct us, provoke us, and fuss at us, at our own request, and so I resent his sneaking sermons in at other times.

10

*Father, help Pat to decide whether or not to accept the call of First Presbyterian Church, and let his decision be made according to the suggestions laid down by Dr. Watershed, in his book,* How to Know God's Will, *which are: (1) . . .*

Prayer by a layperson

I don't mean to imply that only clergy are guilty of preaching in their prayers. This prayer was actually offered in my presence, and it was intended to be supportive to me as I struggled with a decision. I have forgotten the exact title and author of the book she mentioned, but I remember with astonishing clarity that she actually listed the chapter headings by number as she recounted to her Father in Heaven how we are to understand his holy will for our lives. I remember at the time thinking that God must be grateful to her for reviewing this particular volume, so that he would not then have to read it. I ask you: was she praying to God, or to me?

I'll say this for my friend: she was perfectly open in her attempt to coerce me into her point of view. While she was praying, I was sitting in what she called her "Jesus chair," because whoever sat in it soon became conscious that he was being watched by a portrait of our Lord on the wall across from him. "I can tell a lot about a person by the way he acts when he knows Jesus is looking at him," she told me. Also, she used the words "pre-millennial," "post-millennial," and "a-millennial," all in the same sentence, and I had some difficulty keeping up with what they all meant. Her mission in life seems to be one of bringing other people around to the truth, and she really thinks that prayer is one of the legitimate weapons that may be used in such a cause. Tell me, am I guilty of violating Jesus' order not to judge (Matt. 7:1), when I suggest that she is violating Jesus' order not to judge (Matt. 7:1)? I'm not sure on that point, but I do know that I got out of there as soon as possible.

11

*If there is a God, he must surely be omniscient, and hence
he knows already how grateful we are for these gifts.*

Prayer by an agnostic

This was a sort of prayer offered by a friend of mine who is an agnostic, as we sat down to dinner. Actually it was not so much a prayer as an apology to the visiting clergy for the lack of one. But it does contain some of the elements of prayer, and it has at least the virtue of attempted honesty. It *is* an expression of gratitude and humility, which are fundamental necessities of the religious life. It expresses a dependence on food as a gift which comes through forces beyond our control, and it gives evidence of humble delight in receiving it. It also expresses a healthy ignorance about the exact nature of God's existence. This last is surely proper. All prayer should begin with the realization that we do not comprehend God. We are "like" him, in that we are made in his image (Gen. 1:27), but we are forbidden to be "like God, knowing good and evil." These last words were spoken by the serpent (Gen. 3:5), and they are the root temptation that lies at the heart of all human sin.

But, though this blessing has some good elements, it fails as a prayer because of the speaker's belief that God is not personal. If you believe God is not a person then you cannot speak to him, only about him. The speaker is not quite sure on this point because he does use the personal pronoun; if he were certain God were not a person, he should say "it." But to what would the "it" refer? If God is not a person, what is he (it)? Surely he is not simply a "blinding white light" or an amorphous blob like a giant tapioca pudding. Of course God is not like a human, having hands, feet, bears, etc. Such pictures are for children, and adults call them "anthropomorphisms" meaning "having a human form." We don't know what he looks like. But we do know that he is personal. We feel God's presence most clearly in the loving touch of persons, and the one case in history in which Christians say God appeared was in the form of a person. If God is a "force" or "Nature" or anything other than a being who thinks, feels, and wills, then there is no point in praying at all. To pray is to speak to One who can care.

12

*Our Father, we have gathered here this morning from many corners of the world. Some of us have come by automobile; some of us have come by plane; some have come on the railroads; some have ridden the bus, and some of us have walked. Thank you for bringing us safely together.*

From a pastoral prayer

I don't say that this is a bad prayer, unless it is a violation of Matthew 6:7, "Do not heap up empty phrases as the Gentiles do; for they think that they will be heard for their many words." But it makes me uncomfortable that the preacher needs to clarify for God the nature of the various forms of human transportation, as though, in his heavenly distance he is really unaware of the facts of life. Of course it isn't really God whose attention he is trying to get, it is his congregation. He's trying to be a good preacher, and he feels that his prayers have to be eloquent, poetic, and personal. On that last point, I agree with him, and I appreciate his trying to include everybody by listing the available means of conveyance. But why does it have to be flowery and oratorical? What if he began his prayer by speaking honestly to the assembled people rather than to God:

> *I'm glad we have all come together safely, by various means, from all over the world. Let us be silent, giving thanks to God for his care over us as we traveled.*

Then each person can quietly make his or her personal statement of gratitude. The pastor will have served his function: to stimulate us to pray for that which we ought, but which might not have occurred to us. But I don't want to be too hard on him. Leading others in prayer is hard work; few find that rare balance between formality and intimacy that it demands.

*Lord,*
*"Pamper yourself" advertises a local lending agency.*
*Borrow all the money you need, extend yourself.*
*Desires become necessities.*
*It's hard to hear this with one ear, and to hear this*
*quaint word, "deny yourself."*
*Isn't this a bit out-moded?*
*Doesn't it restrict one's freedom to be?*
*Or, is it wisdom which has matured through generations,*
*an enlargement of one's freedom.*
*Self-denial is not giving up candy, or the temporary*
*"giving up" of anything.*
*A self-denial offering is blasphemy—*
*unless, it is a gift from a life which honestly*
*seeks to render permanent control of decisions*
*and purpose to the mind of Christ.*
*"Pamper yourself" or "deny yourself"?*
*I can't escape a choice.*

From a church bulletin

Blasphemy is explaining to God what blasphemy is. Here's another sermon disguised as a prayer. The writer simply took a polemic against self-indulgence (which probably needs to be delivered somewhere), and added the word *Lord,* at the beginning. Does that make it a prayer? If so, it is a singularly arrogant one, explaining to God the meaning of self-denial. I suspect he already knows.

Oh, I know it, I am making a big deal out of a little thing. This isn't really a prayer at all, and the writer isn't guilty of intending all that I impute to him, he's merely guilty of sloppy thinking. But prayers like this, printed on church bulletins and prayed from pulpits, teach young Christians bad habits. No wonder one of them grew up to pray, "Lord, forgive us for intellectual arrogance, which means, Lord,. . . ."

*O Lord, teach me what you would have me to do and help*
*me to do it faithfully and well.*

Daily prayer of a Kentucky man

I have problems with this prayer, even though it fills all of the requirements I have laid down so far: it is brief, simple, non-preachy, free from rhetoric, humble, honest, and committed. Unfortunately, it is too general. That is, it can easily be prayed without making any change in my life. If I set for myself vague standards such as: "I want to be a better person" there will be no way of testing whether I am making any progress toward my goals. In this prayer, I am asking God to improve me, to put me to work, but in such a shadowy and vague way that even if I don't get to work I may never know it.

It is true, of course, that even a specific prayer can have its answer go unrecognized, as in the classic:

*Help, Lord! I'm sliding off the barn roof.*
*Nevermind, Lord, I just hung my britches on a nail.*

But when I am praying for concrete things, I am far more likely to see some concrete progress in my spiritual life. How can this prayer be improved? Well, we all must answer that for ourselves, for the matter is personal, but I could suggest some examples which you would want to change to suit your own life and Christian hopes. You might, for example, pray:

*O Lord, teach me to speak gently to my children when they irritate me,*
*and help me to keep it up.*

or

*O Lord, keep me from winking at that man, I know he's only trouble*
*for me.*

or

*Lord, help me write one more page today, and another one tomorrow.*

Of course, if you truly don't know what God's will for you is, that is another matter, but the problem with most of us is not so much ignorance as lack of motivation.

15

## Goodbye!

This is the shortest and most common prayer of all. We say it so often that we have forgotten it is a prayer. Spoken in full it is "God be with you." In church we call it a *benediction* (from the Latin meaning "to say well.") In most of the places I have worshiped, when the minister raises his hand to bless us he usually looks down at the floor as though he were talking to his shoes, and the people bow their heads. But a benediction is one prayer that is really addressed not only to God but to the earthly folk who hear it as well. "God be with *you!*" You ought to look the preacher in the eye as he asks God to bless you. It is his way of saying "Goodbye" to you after church, and you ought to be saying it back to him. Indeed we ought all to be saying it to each other.

I've always wondered why we only say "Goodbye" when we are leaving. I can think of a number of occasions on which we ought to say, "Goodbye" as we meet: for example, as we gather for a difficult meeting to settle a problem. I think maybe I'll try answering the phone with "Goodbye" for a while and see what kinds of trouble I get into. For that matter, there would be nothing wrong in ending a conversation with "Hello," which means "Health to you!" If *Shalom* can be either a greeting or a parting word (as can *Aloha*), why not "God be with you"?

Note that in this brief phrase we are reminded that the word *God* and the word *good* are related. That's not new. The snake said to Eve that if she ate of the fruit of that tree she would be like "God, knowing good." (Gen. 3:5) And Jesus said, "No one is good but God." (Mark 10:18) The same thing happened as *God's spiel* (good news) became *Godspel* and then *gospel*.

It might be better not to say "Goodbye" unless you mean it. Sometimes, "Beat it!" or "Scram," would be more to the point. It might make enemies, but at least they would know that they could trust us.

## Au secours!

As some wag has suggested, that is either the cry of a drowning Frenchman, or else an unbelievably snobbish American! But in whatever language, "Help" is a basic prayer. You might like to look up the word *help* in a Bible concordance, and pick out those times it occurs in the imperative form of the verb. Quite often it will be easy to spot because it will be the first word in the quotation, and spelled with a capital H. You'll find most of them in the Psalms. If you haven't got a concordance, here are a few such references you can look up:

Psalms 12:1; 79:9; 109:26; Matthew 15:25: these are examples of folk crying out in time of desperation. When you feel like that, either you can't help praying, or, because you have prayed so seldom in good times, you feel shy about praying now that they are tough.

For me a good time to cry out to God with exclamation points is when I am driving the car by myself, preferably with the windows rolled up. Then I can scream "Arrrrgh!" or whatever ultimate groan wants to come out. I remember once simply shouting to God, "This problem is more than I can handle—you're going to have to take over," only the sentence wasn't even grammatical at the time. It was just a cry of anguish. But it was followed by a great peace. And did God really take over the problem? Well, not exactly. He didn't remove it with surgical lightening, but he stood by me, and helped me keep my cool and see it through.

Anyway, "Help!" is a short prayer, and seldom inappropriate. But it is a hard one for those of us who are "self-made men," or "rugged individualists" to pray. First we have to admit we are helpless, and that is not easy.

17

This is a prayer without words. The old adage has it: "He who sings prays twice." And, as one rural elder put it, "He who taps his foot prays three times." Simply to fall to one's knees is to pray with the body. A prayer which is spoken, sung, and danced involves the whole person in communion with God—mind, spirit, and body. Blessed is the one who is well coordinated and can carry a tune.

But all of us can dance, if only to "give a happy hop." And all of us can "make a joyful noise." The tune above is either Handel's "Hallelujah," (if you're high-church) or "Li'l Liza Jane" (if you're low). Try it with the English translation of Hallelujah: "Praise the Lord!"

If, like me, you are shy about singing, do it in your car. Maybe one day you will feel free to do it in the company of other Christians. "To believe in God is to be able to die and not to be embarassed."*

---

*Joseph Pintauro and Sr. Corita Kent, *To Believe in God* (N.Y.: Harper and Row), 1968(n.p.).

*Grant me, O Sacred Heart, a steady hand and watchful eye,*
*That none shall be hurt as I pass by.*
*You gave life—I pray no act of mine*
*Take away or mar that gift Divine.*
*Protect those, dear Lord, who travel with me*
*From highway dangers and all anxiety.*
*Teach me to use my car for other's needs*
*And never to miss through excessive speed the beauty of the world.*
*I pledge to drive with loving concern to my every destination,*
*Offering each travel hour to Thee, in a spirit of Reparation.*
*Most Sacred Heart, my Auto Companion, have mercy on me.*

The Driver's Prayer, revised by Father Gregory
of the Sacred Heart Auto League,
Walls, Mississippi

This prayer came with a Sacred Heart medal to be attached to the windshield, and a membership enrollment blank, inviting me to "share in the Daily Spiritual Benefits of the Apostolate of Prayerful Driving." The brochure explained that the medal had already been blessed, and I was exhorted to "remember the Ninth Promise of the Sacred Heart to St. Margaret Mary: '*I will bless* every place where an image of My Heart is set up and honored.' "

Well, I would agree that prayer is important in the midst of danger, and certainly in today's traffic. And I suspect that a league of "prayerful, careful, reparative drivers" would do as much to reduce highway fatalities as the current national speed limit of 55 miles per hour. But I want to protest that sticking a medal on the windshield is something like repeating a ritual prayer without thinking of it. That won't really help if I drive while drunk, or have bad tires. God doesn't want anybody to perish (Matt. 18:14). That being the case, we are all in his hands, whether we paste prayers on the windshield or not. The next step is to sharpen our compassion for others, discipline our attention to the responsibility of the road, learn to love the countryside, and become better drivers.

*Let there be a revival, Lord, starting with me.*

I have also heard this prayer in slightly different form:

> *Let there be peace on earth*
> *and let it begin with me.*

It is the last phrase that makes it distinctive. It is easy and almost inevitable for people to pray as I often hear:

> *God give us men!*
> or
> *Lord, these are troublous times,*
> or
> *Lord change the world!*

But it is neither easy nor obvious to pray

> *Lord change me.*

Nevertheless, the discipline of prayer, well practiced, must surely bring us to this point at last. Maybe we can formulate a rule something like this:

Pray for the other person's need and for me to have strength to help. But I'm not too sure on this point.

*Lord, give me a gladness*
*that doesn't ignore the world's pain.*

This prayer might better be expressed in the form of a question:

> *Lord, how can I ever celebrate when there is so much suffering around me, and how can I stand it if I don't?*

It seems to me to be the one way of stating life's fundamental question, and that is what makes it a prayer. But you probably will say it a different way. It is possible to put this prayer in very theological terms:

> *Lord keep my mind on both the cross and the resurrection.*

And if you want it in the briefest possible expression, it can come all in the address:

> *O Crucified and Risen Lord.*

On the other hand, if you are naturally informal, your prayer could be something like this:

> *O God who made the Duck-billed Platypus, help me to keep my sense of humor.*

*Lord,*
*Life would be a lot easier if you would leave me alone.*
*In fact, there would be nothing to it.*


This is a prayer that I first prayed, then wrote. Now that I have written it, you can pray it if you want to. There is nothing original about it. It is really no different in intent from Jeremiah 20:7–12. Why then, did I write it down? I think, on reflection, that I was trying to be funny. The prayer contains a fairly subtle pun, turning on the double meaning of the phrase "nothing to it." On the one hand, life without God might be easy; on the other hand, life without God would be utterly empty. (Now that I have explained it, it is certainly no longer funny, if it ever was.)

This raises the question as to whether or not humor has a place in prayer. I think so, but not the kind I am using here. This prayer is really an example of the first problem I raised on page 10 of this book. That is, it isn't really a prayer, it is an epigram. By itself it would look like this:

*There would be nothing to living if God would only stay out of it.*

It may be worth saying once in that form (not twice), but only in order to impress my hearers and help the idea stick in their minds.

God, however, is not going to be impressed with my words, even if they are very clever. Moreover, there is no danger of things not sticking in *his* mind. (See Matthew 6:7–8.) What humor then, if any, would God appreciate? The humor, I believe which is born of humility.* It generally takes the form of confession (Job 42:5–6; 1 Cor. 4:9–10, etc.) and doesn't look much like what we think of as humor. We know, however, that what makes God laugh is human pomposity (Ps. 2:4; 37:13; 59:8), and so I suspect he rejoices when we recognize that in ourselves.

---

*If you're really interested in the relationship of humor to faith, you may want to look at my book *The Gospel According to Andy Capp,* John Knox Press, chapter 10.

*Lord, help me to be real without being obnoxious.*

This prayer sums up for me the essential dilemma of the person who prays in public (or does anything else in public, for that matter). How can you be straightforward and honest, and carry the freight of real personal need, without filling the air with all the pus and poison of human anguish? The very words of this prayer contain a lie. When I first prayed it, I did not use the word *obnoxious*, but a scatalogical term. I have employed the euphemism here since I suspect the publisher would prefer it, and since I don't want to be guilty of trying to be sensational or showy. I have no scruples against four-letter words *per se*. This particular one occurs in the Bible several times (Jer. 8:2; Job 20:7; Mal. 2:3; Phil. 3:8 for example; the K.J.V. is more honest in its translation here than the R.S.V.). But four-letter words should only be used when that is exactly what is meant, never merely for color or emphasis.

Now what do I really mean by this prayer? I mean that every time I open my mouth what I say is colored by my desire to show off, to impress God and my neighbors, by my insecurity, paranoia, delusions of grandeur, compulsiveness, and perfectionism, and all other signs of original sin. Therefore, there is no possible way in which my personal prayers can be honest or very helpful for others. But if, on the other hand, I merely recite the beautiful traditional prayers of the church, because they are free, for the most part, from all these hang-ups, I am not being myself. I dare not leave myself out, lest the prayer be ritualized rote; I dare not put myself in, lest the prayer be my private ego trip. What shall I do? I am trapped. "Who will deliver me from this body of death?" (Rom. 7:24) Only by the miracle of Christ's intercession do my prayers transcend both their public unreality and their private obnoxiousness.

Maybe it would be better simply to say: *"Pray for me Lord; I cannot pray alone."*

23

# III.
# SOME TRADITIONAL PRAYERS

*A few formal, ready-made, prayers serve me as a corrective of—well, let's call it "cheek." They keep one side of the paradox alive. Of course it is only one side. It would be better not to be reverent at all than to have a reverence which denied the proximity.*

C. S. Lewis, *Letters to Malcolm; Chiefly on Prayer* (N.Y.: Harcourt, Brace & World, Inc., 1963), p. 13.

*Now I lay me down to sleep,*
*I pray thee, Lord, my soul to keep.*
*If I should die before I wake,*
*I pray thee, Lord, my soul to take.*

There are some virtues in this old chestnut. It certainly is speaking to a fundamental human concern: the fear of our mortality. It is always appropriate to put yourself into the hands of God, but especially at bed-time, when you shut your eyes and are no longer in charge. Also, it has a kind of sing-song repetitiveness which makes it easy to remember. As a child I said it every night before going to sleep, although I generally changed the last verse and prayed:

*Help me to be kind and good,*
*And to love thee as I should.*

I think that I substituted this couplet because I didn't like to reflect regularly on my death. It seemed a morbid thing for a small boy to be doing, and I felt that the prayer needed to be more than supplication for my own needs, but ought to reach out in some ethical responsibility. Apparently we get the idea very early that God's grace can't really be trusted and we have to add some responsibility of our own to assuage the guilt feelings.

As I say, this is not a bad prayer. "We are always being given up to death" (2 Cor. 4:11) so we always need to be prepared for it, and we have a good example for saying, "Father, into thy hands I commit my spirit." (Luke 23:46) But I am suspicious of prayer that is doggerel. Of the relationship between prayer and poetry we will have more to say, but this isn't poetry, it is merely rhyme. It may be helpful to enable children to remember it, but for an adult to pray like this is almost as unreal as the star of a musical comedy breaking into song to his lover. Good theatrics, perhaps, but questionable in real life. I have long been grateful that the Psalms do not rhyme; this makes them translatable into any language without altering the text; perhaps here is another reason.

*God is great, God is good,*
*And we thank him for our food.*

This one doesn't even rhyme, unless you mispronounce either *good* or *food*. Therefore it irritates my aesthetic sense, but I have to admit it is not without some virtues:

In the first place, it is brief and to the point.

Second, it is straightforward and honest.

Third, it follows an ancient form of prayer which the church has found helpful through the centuries: namely to give one or two of God's attributes as we approach him. This is not in order to explain things to God, or to impress him, but to *praise*, which is the natural function of religious persons, and to establish a mind-set which will help us pray. You are familiar with examples of this:

> *Almighty God, unto whom all hearts are open . . .*
> *Merciful Father . . .*
> *Eternal God . . .*
> *Our Father, who art in heaven . . .*

But in addition to being doggerel, this prayer bothers me because it isn't really addressed to God. What's wrong with that? Plenty of the Psalms are written in the third person:

> *The Lord is my shepherd . . .*
> *Praise the Lord, all nations!*

I think, strictly speaking, that such poems are not really prayers but hymns or doxologies. They are proper as acts of praise or devotion, but as patterns for prayer they tend to develop in us the habit of talking *about* God instead of *to* him. In that sense this little prayer is a theological dissertation. It says something about God's majesty, and his essential benevolence, and then it says that we ought to be grateful. But it is not in itself an act of gratitude. I think before I would recommend "God is great" as a table-blessing I would cast my vote for a fervent prayer I heard once from a little Episcopal lady. She sat down at the table and said, "Boy, am I hungry!" "Amen," we all said, and fell to. No theology in that, but a lot of gratitude.

*Come, Lord Jesus, be our guest,*
*And may this food by thee be blest.*

Old German table grace

Only God knows how many invocations have been prayed by the church. "Come, Holy Spirit . . . ," "Be present with us O Lord. . . ." I have been asked to "give the invocation" at football games, psychiatrist's gatherings, civic clubs, and dances, even once at an association of private detectives! But I have never done it without having the fleeting thought: Why am I doing this? Why should we ever ask God to come? Isn't he always here? Is he some genie in a bottle that we can conjure him up by proper incantation? Shouldn't the prayer really rather be:

*Lord Jesus, you are our guest!*
or
*Holy Spirit, make us receptive to you.*

And yet on second thought, if we can pray at all, isn't this the fundamental prayer? Perhaps the oldest liturgical formula known to the church is the old Aramaic word *maranatha,* "Come Lord Jesus." It is found in 1 Corinthians 16:22, and it is the prayer with which the Bible ends (Rev. 22:20). It is not that we can make Jesus come by our prayers; it is rather that the discipline of praying for his coming is a way of acknowledging our need for him, and in that sense making ourselves receptive. So, in a way, he does come when we call. Not that he can be manipulated, but that only in calling him do we apprehend his presence. It is the old catch: righteousness only comes to those who know they are not righteous (Matt. 5:6); the gift cannot be mine unless I am willing to receive it.

I know of a family who kept an empty chair at the breakfast table to symbolize that Jesus has a place in their house. When I first heard of this I laughed. But then it occurred to me that if that empty chair could be filled with a hungry person off the street, or that extra meal delivered to a needy soul, or the money it would cost sent to the starving half of the world, he would be with us indeed (Matt. 25:40).

*Matthew, Mark, Luke, John!*
*Bless the bed that I lie on!*


This old prayer is almost a joke. I remember a fire-breathing evangelist excoriating a congregation for their shallow faith by telling a horrible tale of travelers surrounded by cannibals beating their drums. When in their last extremity they decided to pray, this was the only prayer any of them knew! I admit that's a pretty bad prayer for such an emergency. It is in a class with:

> *Good bread! Good meat!*
> *Good God! Let's eat!*

But if there is anything good in it at all, I want to praise it. Because I happen to think that even a fumbling, bad prayer by an honest layman, attempting to put his faith to work at last, is worth all the flowery phrases of the best professional Christian that ever lived (Luke 15:7).

Is there anything good in this prayer? Well, it makes the mistake of addressing itself to the four evangelists, rather than the Source of the Good News Himself. But that is an honest mistake. A new Christian quite often falls into the trap of turning to his preacher, or his Christian friends, for help that only God can give. Is this altogether bad? Did not Jesus promise his disciples that they would do even greater work than he (John 14:12)? And aren't we promised power even to unlock the chains of guilt that bind people, and set them free from their sins (Matt. 16:19)? It is good to know that we have access directly to God through Jesus Christ, but sometimes (if not nearly always) this way is unlocked by a Christian friend, or one of the Bible writers like the four mentioned in this prayer.

Moreover, I like the common touch of blessing the bed. Once I took part in an Episcopal ceremony blessing a whole house (except we skipped the bathroom). A lot of it was over my liturgical head, and I felt a little foolish, but I had to admit that the idea was a healthy one. A lot of bedrooms could use a blessing. What about kitchens, pantries, laundries, garages, and guest rooms (2 Kings 4:8–10)? Or even living rooms?

*Lord, make me an instrument of Thy peace.*
　*Where there is hatred, let me sow love;*
　*Where there is injury, pardon;*
　*Where there is doubt, faith;*
　*Where there is despair, hope;*
　*Where there is darkness, light;*
　*And where there is sadness, joy.*
*O Divine Master, grant that I may not so much seek to be*
　*consoled as to console;*
*To be understood as to understand;*
*To be loved as to love;*
　*For it is in giving that we receive,*
*It is in pardoning that we are pardoned,*
*And it is in dying that we are born to eternal life.*

St. Francis of Assisi

I suppose this prayer has helped as many people as any outside the Bible itself, so it is with temerity that I offer any criticism at all. But it does seem to me to suffer from two things. The first and most flagrant fault is the last paragraph. The good saint (there are bad saints, too, don't forget) has slipped a little sermonette in at the end of his prayer. His advice is eminently correct; Jesus said almost exactly the same thing after offering his disciples The Lord's Prayer (Matt. 6:14–15). But there it is clear that he had ceased to address his Father in heaven and was instructing his disciples. If that is what Assisi meant, why not include the last paragraph as a footnote? Certainly God doesn't need to be told how his own mercy operates.

My other problem with it is harder to get hold of. I think it is slightly tainted with rehtoric—that is, it sounds as though it was written with an ear to the aesthetic appreciation it might arouse in its audience. It is very hard to do that and still maintain perfect honesty before God. But of course we are now dealing with a matter of taste, and *de gustibus non est disputandum*. (When the bus is drafty, some want to close the windows, and some want to open them.)

30

*Almighty and most merciful Father: We have erred, and
strayed from thy ways like lost sheep. We have followed
too much the devices and desires of our own hearts. We
have offended against thy holy laws. We have left undone
those things which we ought to have done; And we have
done those things which we ought not to have done; And
there is no health in us. But Thou, O Lord, have mercy
upon us, miserable offenders.*

*The Book of Common Prayer*

This is a tough old prayer; most Episcopalians (and many of the rest of us)
have sharpened their confessing skill upon it. But it is hard to take. There is
something in us that wants to cry out, "I am *not* a miserable offender!" Surely
there is some good, even in the worst of us. How can we say, "There is no health
in us"? Isn't this a kind of self-defeating pessimism? Maybe so, but it has good
company: the Psalmist who bemoaned, "There is none that does good, no, not
one," (14:3) and the Apostle Paul: "I know that nothing good dwells within me."
(Rom. 7:18) Compared to the standard set for us all by Jesus ("Be perfect") in
the Sermon on the Mount, we are lost sheep.

We have a hard time accepting this. In one congregation there was a real
controversy over the wording of a general confession which said, "we have hated
our neighbors and been unkind to our families." One woman refused to say it,
but she approached the minister with a suggested solution. "All we have to do,"
she said, "to settle this controversy, is change the pronouns to say 'we confess
that *they* have hated *their* neighbors, etc.'" That would do it all right.

Another solution would be simply not to take human sin very seriously, and
pray as David Head suggested:

"Benevolent and easy-going Father: . . . We have done the best we could in
the circumstances. . . ."*

But the best way is to meet the crusty old prayer head on, change the ancient
Elizabethan to Contemporary English if we like, but not alter its fundamental
willingness to face the truth.

---

*\*He Sent Leanness* (N.Y.: Macmillan, 1959), p. 19.

*O Lord, support us all the day long of this troublous life, until the shadows lengthen, and the evening comes, and the busy world is hushed, and the fever of life is over, and our work is done. Then, in thy mercy, grant us a safe lodging, and holy rest, and peace at the last; through Jesus Christ our Lord.*

John Henry Newman

The Cardinal's prayer has touched thousands of hearts, and I hesitate to talk about it. But some things need to be said; let us see to it that we make an omelet if we break any eggs. This prayer is really not intended for funerals, though that is where you usually hear it. It is a prayer for living—for the painful process of getting from breakfast to bed-time. And its very strength lies in its rhetoric. It conjures up a vision of peace, security, and eternal rest. I suspect it is a popular prayer for the same reason that *Abide with Me* continues to be one of the best-loved hymns in America. As a "hart panteth after the water brooks" (Ps. 42:1 K.J.V.) and as a weary soldier longs for a halt, so the Christian in the troubled world dreams of rest at last.

It is not a bad dream. I would never fault any honest soul for enjoying the thought of coming at last to the end. It's just that to concentrate altogether on the rest at evening is to miss the point of the day. The day's significance lies in the toil, not in the rest. The rest, indeed, becomes a glad rest precisely because of the weary work that precedes it. So I wish the Cardinal had used as much poetry in describing "this troublous life" as he did in talking about the peace at the last.

I wouldn't presume to re-write this classic. So let me suggest another one, to be prayed in the morning:

*Lord, you worked for six days, and then rested. Give me gladness in my labor, kindness in my words. Let me do good as I pass this way, and rest easy at the end, through Jesus Christ.*

But that doesn't quite do it. Try your hand at it.

*O Thou who hast ordered this wondrous world and who knowest all things in earth and heaven: So fill our hearts with trust in Thee that by night and by day, at all time and in all seasons, we may without fear commit those who are dear to us to Thy never-failing love for this life and the life to come.*

From the Funeral Service

There have been some modern versions of this prayer, but it is one so laden with emotional content for me that I have kept it here in Elizabethan English for the sheer joy of the sound of it. That is probably a dangerous thing to do. When a prayer begins to sound "pretty" apart from the meaning of the words, it has taken the first step toward becoming a soothing cover-up that prevents honest confrontation with God and myself. It may be better to err in the direction of a prayer that is pure emotion rather than pure intellect, for in the long run the heart is more powerful than the head. But it is even better to have both. So perhaps you would like this prayer as the 1970 edition of *The Worshipbook* (p. 87) has it:

*O God: you have designed this wonderful world, and know all things good for us. Give us such faith that, by day and by night, in all times and in all places, we may without fear trust those who are dear to us to your never-failing love, in this life and the life to come.*

I don't know why *designed* is better than *ordered*, or *trust* is better than *commit*, but I do see the value of dropping antique verb forms such as *knowest*, which you rarely hear in ordinary conversation. In so far as we can pray in words that help us feel that we are actually making conversation to God, it will help our prayers ring with reality. Of course, if you can speak naturally in Elizabethan (and some people can) then you have my permission to do so, but if you are going to lead in public prayer, remember that a lot of your congregation is accustomed to think: "Oh, I thought you were just praying, I didn't know you really meant anything."

33

*Here we are, our Father.*
*You called us, and we've come.*
*You want us to learn some more about your love for us,*
*and we want your help to make our lives less selfish and*
*more loving.*
*So we have come to church*
*to listen to what you have to say to us,*
*to give you thanks for what you do for us*
*and to share with you the hopes you have given us*
*through Jesus.*
*Help us to make good use of our time together:*
*and when we leave here again help us to take our*
*worship home with us.*
*Through Jesus Christ our Lord.*

An Opening Prayer (Especially when children are present)*

I have included this prayer because it is a good one, and because it illustrates an important point: prayers composed with children in mind will usually speak to adults; the converse is not true. There is a difference between being *childish*, which we are warned to put away (2 Corinthians 13:11) and *childlike*, which we are enjoined to become (Matt. 18:3–4). To be like a child is to demonstrate openness, trust, honesty, and above all a sense of wonder. It is when we are trying the hardest to act "grown-up" that we are most likely to be childish. (How many boys have thought it "grown-up" to smoke cigarettes when it is really reverting to a pacifier!) Therefore, if we are to write childlike prayers we will keep them simple, straightforward, expectant, and down to earth, as the prayer above is. If we would only apply the same rules for writing prayers for adults, or for praying our own prayers, we would slough off a great deal of useless phraseology, and the result would be meat that adults might chew.

*Caryl Micklem, ed., *Contemporary Prayers for Public Worship* (London: SCM Press Ltd, 1967), p. 26.

*Almighty God, who through thine only-begotten Son Jesus Christ overcame death, and opened to us the gate of everlasting life: Grant that we, who celebrate with joy the solemnity of the Lord's resurrection, may arise from the death of sin through the renewal of your Holy Spirit; through Jesus Christ our Lord, who now lives and reigns with you and the Holy Spirit, one God, for ever and ever.*

Collect for Easter Day
*Services for Trial Use* 1971, p.527

*Services for Trial Use* is a book born of the enormous courage and dedication to liturgy of the Episcopal Church. They take worship very seriously indeed, and while this may lead to undue pomposity, and mistaking of human dignity for reverence, it also leads to the most moving and relevant liturgical experiences. Only in the very high or the very low churches are the depths of emotions plumbed. For that reason the phrase "miserable offenders" can be read with passion by an Anglican, or spoken with spontaneous sincerity by a Black Baptists, but most worshiping WASPS are unable to deal with our guilt. (Have you ever wondered why the *Amen* is present at both ends of the liturgical spectrum but often missing in the middle?)

The quest for "solemn joy" contained in the central petition is one way of stating the basic quest of this book: that we learn to pray with both reverence and delight. Every Sunday is for the Christian a little Easter. We worship on the first day of the week precisely because it is the anniversary of the resurrection. Among all the delicious implications of that fact, one is surely that we do not remain at the cross, as central to our faith as it is, but move beyond it to the happy ending.

The phrase with which the prayer ends is an ancient formula which helps us remember the three-fold nature of the God to whom we pray. You probably wouldn't ordinarily use such formal words in your private devotions, for they are the language of ceremony, but they are good words, and can help prevent any tendency to see God in a narrow way.

35

*Silence*

An empty page for you to use in writing your own prayer (or to criticize this book, or to use however you like). Empty pages are sort of like silence: they are a little frightening, but they are very useful, and incredibly rare. (I'd better get quiet, or this one won't be empty.)

## Amen.*

Strictly speaking, *Amen* is not part of the prayer itself, although most people think so. If you don't believe this, try leaving it off of the table grace at your next formal banquet and watch the awkward glancing around of people who are asking, "Is it over?" We think that *Amen* means *The end*, because that's where it usually comes, and we seem to need it in church as a cue for the organist to start the postlude or the next hymn. But *Amen*, one of the few Hebrew words most English speaking people know, is properly translated, "Right on!" (Or, of course, "Me too," "my sentiments exactly," "so mote [must] it be.") Properly, the word belongs not to the priest, but to the people. The preacher ought not to say it unless he is responding to something the congregation has said, or when he wishes to reaffirm, or underscore something, or to say, at the end of the sermon, for instance, "I've done my best, let that stand." Ordinarily it ought not be sung at the end of hymns, since it is redundant, and implies that somehow we didn't really mean it the first time. (Of course, in some hymns the *Amen* is musically necessary since the composer was unaware of the point I am making.)

In low churches, *Amens* are spontaneous responses from the people when they affirm the preacher; in high churches, *Amens* are programmed responses from the people when the book tells them to say it. In my ideal church (which I am going to found as soon as I can find 12 ideal Christians) the *Amen* will be proper in both ways. (I think also if we're going to have an *Amen* corner we ought also to have an *O Yeah?* corner for those who disagree with the sermon or other parts of the worship.)

There is a sense of course in which, all by itself, *Amen* can be a fervent prayer, an acceptance of the universe, a commitment of trust to the process, a way of saying to God, "Whatever you have in store for me, let it happen!" (Rev. 22:20)

*How do you pronounce it? Either way. "Ah-men" sounds prettier musically; "Aye-men" is a stronger word. Take your pick. I sometimes say it one way, sometimes the other.

# IV.
## PRAYERS FROM HEBREW HISTORY

*Then Jacob awoke from his sleep and said, "Surely the Lord is in this place; and I did not know it." And he was afraid, and said, "How awesome is this place! This is none other than the house of God, and this is the gate of heaven."*

Genesis 28: 16–17

*I heard the sound of thee in the garden, and I was afraid, because I was naked; and I hid myself.*

Adam (Genesis 3:10)

If prayer, by definition, is a person speaking to God, then this is the first prayer, for it is the first recorded word spoken by Adam to his Creator. (We do know, of course, that he named all the beasts, and that he uttered a thanksgiving to nobody in particular when his wife was created [2:23]. But this is the first word specifically addressed to God.)

a. It was prayed in a garden, which may be of some comfort to those who think that's the best place to pray.

b. It was at least honest; he had learned to cheat and hide, but he had not yet learned to lie.

c. It was spoken in quivering terror, not in the cathedral calm that we associate with devotional moods.

d. It was not originated by Adam, but was a response to God's call. God initiated this prayer by calling to Adam. (We often get confused on this, asking "How can I find God?" The question we ought to be asking is, "How can God find me?")

e. It is fraught with self-pity and a desire to avoid blame. The next response by Adam clearly passes the buck: " 'The woman whom thou gavest to be with me, she gave me fruit of the tree, and I ate.' " (Gen. 3:12) (The woman of course passed the blame on to the serpent.)

f. It is full of false modesty. By what logic need a naked man hide from God in a bush? God can see through bushes, and clothes, and alibis, and everything else. It is for our own sake that we need to wear clothes. Isn't it strange that the first result of eating of the fruit of the tree of knowledge would be a sexual hang-up? As long as, like children, they basked in innocence, their nakedness went unnoticed. But when they began to develop an ethic (know good and evil), they believed themselves to be ridiculous. No wonder Bonhoeffer wrote, "The knowledge of good and evil seems to be the aim of all ethical reflection. The first task of Christian ethics is to invalidate this knowledge."*

*Ethics* (N.Y.: Macmillan, 1965), p. 17.

*Oh let not the Lord be angry, and I will speak again but this once. Suppose ten are found there.*

Abram (Genesis 18:32)

This is the last petition in a long argument between Abram and God. It starts out with the Lord's announcement that he will destroy Sodom, and Abram's request that the city be spared if there are as many as fifty righteous people there. When this is granted, he asks for forty-five, then forty, thirty, twenty, and finally ten. Apparently he decided that he had pushed his luck far enough.

The trouble with arguing in prayer to God is not simply that it is impolite or presumptuous for me to do so, " 'I who am but dust and ashes.' " (Gen. 18:27) The whole idea of prayer is itself presumptuous. No, the trouble lies in the fact that God might give in and grant what we ask! He usually does, you know (Mark 11:24), and sometimes it is not at all as nice as we thought. Somebody has called this "God's terrible OK." My father, when he was a child, admired his friends' goat cart, and prayed night after night for a billy-goat. Then one glorious morning he looked out in the back yard and there stood the answer to his prayers. With open arms he ran to greet his new goat, who lowered his head and ran to meet my father. The less said about the resulting encounter, the better.

Probably it is a good idea to plead your case before God with utter stubbornness. But just make sure what you are praying so passionately for is what you really want. You may get it. Pray for success, and the "Peter principle" will find you at last at your level of incompetence; pray for a certain girl to marry, and you find that living with her is not at all what you expected; pray for what you call heaven, and it might turn out to be hell. Perhaps the best prayer is: "God, give me heaven, whatever that means!"

*By myself I have sworn.*

Does God ever pray? Well, yes. Indeed there is a sense in which only God can pray. I cannot pray unless his Spirit moves me. "No one can say 'Jesus is Lord' except by the Holy Spirit." (1 Cor. 12:3) To whom then does God pray? To himself. In that sense he prays just like the rest of us. Prayer is the art of seeing myself through the eyes of God; hence knowing reality. For what does God pray? Well, here are some examples:

> "I desire steadfast love and not sacrifice." (Hos. 6:6)
>
> " 'Whom shall I send, and who will go for us?' " (Isa. 6:8)
>
> "Let justice roll down like waters, and righteousness like an ever-flowing stream." (Amos 5:24)
>
> " 'O Jerusalem, Jerusalem, killing the prophets and stoning those who are sent to you! How often would I have gathered your children together as a hen gathers her brood under her wings, and you would not!' " (Matt. 23:37)

God longs for his people to be obedient, holy, loving, and united. As Paul summarizes it, "He chose us in him before the foundation of the world, that we should be holy and blameless before him. He destined us in love to be his sons through Jesus Christ, according to the purpose of his will . . . as a plan for the fulness of time, to unite all things in him, things in heaven and things on earth." (Eph. 1:4–5, 10)

Of course, there is a sense in which God (seen as philosophical absolute) has no need of anything (Acts 17:25), but apparently God values relationships more than absolutes. That is why we talk about him as a "trinity." He contains relationship within himself, for he is Love (1 John 4:8). Because he is Love, he longs for the beloved, and desires her (Jer. 31:31–34; Rev. 21:2, 9–10). As an earthly parent looses the apron strings that her child may grow up, to be loved on a deeper level, so God permits us to walk out of his love, but he is ever the waiting Father (Luke 15:20) who longs for our safe return. For that God prays. And by his own name he has sworn an oath to keep his covenant.

42

*The Lord watch between you and me, when we are absent one from the other.*

Laban (Genesis 31:49)

I don't know how many times I have stood in a circle of young people or adults, joined hands (often with the arms crossed), and repeated the "Mizpah Benediction." Here is an example of words that carry freight they never intended. In context, of course, this is more of a warning than a blessing. It is spoken by Laban, Jacob's uncle, who has been stolen blind by his nephew, and is desperately glad to be getting rid of him. It is time for Jacob to depart, taking Laban's children, his grandchildren, his herds, and a few household idols (which Rachel sat on, thereby preventing a search of her person by claiming to be menstruating; see 31:34–35). All in all it is not a very happy domestic scene, and the covenant (agreement) which Jacob and his uncle make is designed to keep them from further entanglement. Laban agrees to let Jacob go, with the promise that he won't mistreat his daughters, or marry any other wives. And, as a sign of this, they erect a pile of stones, which Laban calls "Mizpah" meaning "watchpost," saying, in effect,

*May the Lord keep a sharp eye on you when you're out of my sight.*

Now the question must be faced: so what if this "benediction" *is* often used out of context? Don't the people who use it really mean it as a blessing, and is it really important that the words originally meant something else, if they are now a sincere expression of mutual concern? Well, you have a point, and I continue to say this prayer with feeling when called upon. Surely it is better for words to gain extra meaning rather than to lose meaning (see *hocus-pocus* on page 86). But one of the essentials for good praying that is emerging for me in this study is a passion for truth. And if this prayer is a kind of reversal of the original meaning of the words, aren't we in some danger here?

*If I come to the people of Israel and say to them, "The God of your fathers has sent me to you," and they ask me, "What is his name?" what shall I say to them?*

Moses (Exodus 3:13)

*Who are you, Lord?*

Paul (Acts 9:5)

How do you pray if you don't know God's name? There is a sense, of course, in which that is completely unnecessary. You don't need to know the lifeguard's name to shout, "Help!" Every heartfelt prayer is heard by God, though it be badly worded or even wrongly addressed. But there is another sense in which it is absolutely essential. "There is no other name under heaven given among men by which we must be saved." (Acts 4:7–12) The name which God gave to Moses in answer to his question was I AM, so that the Hebrews called him Yahweh, the one who is. To know God's name is to understand what is, to know the nature of reality. And to know reality is to be able to be honest with yourself. One definition of prayer is just that: ultimate awareness.

The answer to Paul's question is, " 'I am Jesus, whom you are persecuting.' " (Acts 9:5) The guilt over his frenzied attack on the Christians has finally built up in Paul until at last, in blindness and terror, he is forced to face the truth about himself: he has been fighting the very thing he sought; he has been fleeing from the very hope of heaven.

To pray in the name of Jesus means to confront the reality of a universe which is grounded in grace, and where the secret of finding life is in losing it. When I bring before him my pretensions or my fears, I find that I must give up the former, and that I may give up the latter. In either case I come away cleansed. To encounter the surgeon-knife of reality, however painful, is to come away cured. To pray to a lesser or false deity, is, in the long run, to worsen my disease, even though I may feel better for the moment.

But if I do not know who God is when I begin to pray, the proper thing (as with Moses and Paul) is to ask. Honest ignorance gets me off to a better start than the wrong sort of piety.

*Sing to the LORD, for he has triumphed gloriously;*
*the horse and his rider he has thrown into the sea.*

Miriam (Exodus 15:21)

Some prayer is pure joy! This is really the chorus of a spontaneous song, got up by Moses and the people of Israel after their remarkable deliverance through the Red Sea. In good operatic style the whole assembly sang a glad hymn to the One who had drowned the Egyptians. Then Miriam, a female clergy-person, and Moses' sister, grabbed up a tamborine and started a procession of dancing women who sang this chorus. I'm not sure about the good taste of this couplet; I mean, singing over a drowned army, even if they are your enemy, has gone out of style in a more genteel age. But it was like a cheer in the stands at a football game when a certain defeat is turned into victory. It couldn't be helped, it came from the soul, and you don't question a person's taste under conditions like that. It is one of the earliest examples of Hebrew poetry.

How can you possibly compare the ecstatic song of a jubilant prophetess with what happens in our churches today? With, for example, the Collect for Purity from the *Book of Common Prayer:*

> *Almighty God, unto whom all hearts are open, all desires known,*
> *and from whom no secrets are hid; Cleanse the thoughts of our hearts*
> *by the inspiration of thy Holy Spirit, that we may perfectly love thee,*
> *and worthily magnify thy holy Name; through Christ our Lord.* *

Well, of course you can't. The one is a primitive yell of victory, the other, a finely tuned expression of the church's liturgy at its best. To compare them is as absurd as a child's asking, "Daddy is it as cold on Thursday as it is in the dining room?" But there is a relationship: if you have been disciplined in proper liturgy, by learning such collects as this one, when you are suddenly surprised by a shouting situation, your spontaneous prayer will be far more likely to express what you really mean.

---

*"The Order for the Administration of the Lord's Supper or Holy Communion" in *The Book of Common Prayer* (N.Y.: Morehouse-Gorham Co., 1938), p. 67.

*O LORD God, remember me, I pray thee, and strengthen me, I pray thee, only this once, O God, that I may be avenged upon the Philistines for one of my two eyes.*

Samson (Judges 16:28)

There is a saying, "There are no atheists in foxholes," which is generally meant as an insult to those who finally get religion when the situation gets bad enough. But, sisters and brothers, that's the way it is. For Prodigal Sons it gets bad in one way, and for Elder Brothers it gets bad in another, but it is not necessarily paradise (as Adam discovered) that leads people to God, it is whatever forces us to face up to our finitude. That may be a colossal sense of God's goodness and love, but we tend to take all that for granted until some devastataion forces us back on the ground of our being. God, in his mercy, brings troubles on us, because he loves us, and sometimes it is the only way we can be brought round (Rev. 3:19).

Apparently nothing but utter disaster could get through to Samson. All his life he had been a spoiled kid and a bully, taking what he wanted and teasing everybody with riddles in the process. He was so big and strong that he fell into the trap that faces all successful people: forgetting that his powers were gifts from God. At last, he went the way of so many whose gifts seem to destroy them: F. Scott Fitzgerald, Jackson Pollock, Hank Williams. Someone has suggested that the saddest line in all of literature is that from *Samson Agonistes:* "Eyeless in Gaza, at the mill with slaves." (I would vote for Ephesians 2:12.) There at the end of all things, he cries in agony to God for one more chance. And it comes. In one final heroic act he is delivered from the life-long nemesis of his strength, and is placed in the rank of heroes. It is truly a miracle.

It may be a bad prayer, full of selfishness and revenge, but it worked. Thus may you and I pray, however badly, in our moment, and expect a miracle.

46

*O LORD of hosts, if thou wilt indeed look on the affliction of thy maidservant, and remember me, and not forget thy maidservant, but wilt give to thy maidservant a son, then I will give him to the LORD all the days of his life, and no razor shall touch his head.*

Hannah (1 Samuel 1:11)

Hannah's prayer brought her peace, but it raises some problems with her theology. It is a violation of the rule stated in Deuteronomy 6:16, " 'You shall not put the LORD your God to the test,' " which Jesus quoted to the devil at the temptation. And even if God were susceptible to this kind of bargaining, a number of difficulties are raised. The principal one is what you have locked yourself into by praying this way. Many youngsters, moved by adolescent guilt, have said something like this:

God, get me out of this mess, and I'll be a missionary.

Unless that turns out in fact to be the best vocation for him, he'll either be a miserable round peg in a square hole, or haunted by a vow not kept. Unless, of course he can think as fast as that airline passenger in the storm to whom a priest said, "I heard you promise God if he got you out of this you'd give him a thousand dollars, and I'll be glad to help you fulfil your vow." "No thanks, Father," he said. "I made him an even better deal. I told him that if I ever got back on one of these things I'd give him all the money I had."

As it turned out, Hannah did get a son, and Samuel did turn out to be a mighty prophet before the Lord. But even more important than that, her prayer brought an end to her depression. (E.g. verses 10 and 18.) It is poorly worded and theologically unsound, but fundamentally it has done the right thing: turn the problem over to God. As Peter advises us, "Cast all your anxieties on him, for he cares about you." (1 Pet. 5:7) Also the boy must have saved a small fortune on barber bills.

*Speak, Lord, for thy servant hears.*

Samuel (1 Samuel 3:10)

One of the problems with having a very religious mother (I can tell you from experience) is that you practically live at the church. Samuel in fact did live there, and eventually he heard God speak. It is not true that God is more likely to speak in church than elsewhere, any more than it is true that you are nearer to God's heart in a garden than anywhere else on earth. But it is probably true that you are more likely to hear him there for what our fathers called "the means of grace" are available: the interpretation of the Scriptures and the Sacraments. There too, prayer is given formal expression, and one is expected either to take part, or to bow reverently and listen.

Now it is this last that is the hard part. Every possible distraction will rear its head. Even absolute silence can be bothersome, which prompted someone to say "that a railway compartment, if one has it to oneself, is an extremely good place to pray in 'because there is just the right amount of distraction.' "* But, whatever the surroundings, cathedral or garden, listening is hard work. Being in church can work either way. It can help you sharpen your listening skills, or it can dull you to the point of blocking out all heavenly sounds. It was, after all, the leading religious folk of his day that had the hardest time hearing Jesus.

The important thing is to listen—really listen. Usually we don't. Usually we spend all our energy talking, and we filter whatever replies we get through our wish-fulfillment or our fears. But the overwhelming majority of conversations in the Bible between God and man are initiated by God. Indeed, what makes Judeo-Christianity different from the religions of the world is that our faith is not about man's search for God, but his search for us.

He that has ears to hear, let him hear.

*C. S. Lewis, *Letters to Malcolm* (N.Y.: Harcourt, Brace & World, 1963), p. 18.

*O LORD my God, thou hast made thy servant king in place of David my father, although I am but a little child; I do not know how to go out or come in. Give thy servant therefore an understanding mind to govern thy people, that I may discern between good and evil; for who is able to govern this thy great people?*

Solomon (1 Kings 3:7,9)


God's response to this prayer was to tell Solomon that because he had not asked for riches, but for understanding, he would be given both. Of course Solomon dreamed the whole thing (3:15), but that's the way it turned out. It looks as though this is a sneaky way to get what we want from God: like asking Santa for new clothes when what we really want is a bicycle. It also looks as though Jesus' fundamental principle can be used the same way: "Whoever loses his life will find it," so the thing to do is act humble and then you'll get great. But not so. There is a catch (indeed, it is Catch One). And the catch is that you really have to lose your life; you can't pretend to lose it, figuring you'll really find it after all. If Solomon had lied in praying for wisdom, when what he really wanted was cash, it wouldn't have worked.

The reason for this is a fundamental fact of life which we never seem to remember: virtue is its own reward. To serve is to reign. To become God's servant is to find perfect freedom. To empty myself is to become full. It's simply too incredible, so the world rejects it. But every time you lean on it, it supports you. When you give to God a child who is about to have surgery, the child may die or live, but in either case the ending is bearable—that is if you really did give him up. Am I saying become an ascetic—and give up all worldly goods? No (actually there are no worldly goods; only God is good), I'm saying worldly goods can never be enjoyed until they have been given up. Like children, they are only fun for their parents when we let them leave home.

49

*My father, my father!*
*the chariots of Israel and its horsemen!*

Elisha (2 Kings 2:12)

It was just after dawn when the bedside phone awakened me with news of my father's death. And as I hung up, that haunting cry of Elisha intruded itself on my consciousness. I wonder why. I don't even know what the words mean. They were a burst of poetry in the midst of an experience words cannot describe. The fiery Elijah had vanished in flames—what was Elisha to think or say? Is it necessary that we understand our prayers? Well, no, if they are private. When we are speaking publicly, "I would rather speak five words with my mind, in order to instruct others, than ten thousand words in a tongue." (1 Cor. 14:19) But there is a place for ecstatic expression addressed to God (14:39); he understands utterances whose freight is too heavy for words.

There is nothing glib to say when your father or mother dies. The fearful awareness of one's mortality, the staggering weight of the mantle of history, the joyful liberation of being at last grown up, and the guilty nagging of past failures, all shout to be heard. There is nothing to talk about but fiery chariots and horsemen. It is your own death that you fear, in such a time, and it takes more than poetry to translate that fiery vision into a "sweet chariot."

I have said that this is a cry beyond words, and yet I keep on talking about it. I believe I'll stop.

*O my son Absalom, my son, my son Absalom!*
*Would I had died instead of you.*
*O Absalom, my son, my son!*

David (2 Samuel 18:33)

This prayer is not addressed to God, but in such an hour who will pick at so small a nit? Prayers can be addressed to anyone, or anything. ("Sweet Hour of Prayer," is addressed to a time of day.) Just be sure that you are clear on which God you really worship. One of the problems of David's grief is a tendency to worship Absalom rather than give him up (see the discussion under Solomon's prayer). You may well ask, how can one not be completely wrapped up in a son when he dies? It is almost impossible not to. That is why affection is more dangerous than lust. "The false religion of lust is baser than the false religion of mother-love or patriotism or art: but lust is less likely to be made into a religion."*

But, believe it or not, it *is* possible to lose a son and still believe in ultimate goodness and mercy. God himself did this, they say. And I can't help thinking of Stephen Kumalo, whose son (also named Absalom) was executed in the South African dawn. But as the old man grieved, crying like David, " 'My son, my son, my son,' " his heart went out to all the people of Africa, the beloved country. " '*Nkosi Sikelel' iAfrika,* ' " he prayed, "God save Africa." None of us can turn it all loose yet, but in Christ the light has dawned. "Yes it is the dawn that has come. The titihoya wakes from sleep, and goes about its work of forlorn crying. The sun tips with light the mountains of Ingeli and East Griqualand. The great valley of the Umzimkulu is still in darkness, but the light will come there."**

---

*C. S. Lewis, *The Great Divorce* (N.Y.: Macmillan, 1962), p. 99.
**Alan Paton, *Cry, the Beloved Country* (N.Y.: Scribner's, 1948 , pp. 275–7.

51

*So all Israel brought up the ark of the covenant of the LORD with shouting, to the sound of the horn, trumpets, and cymbals, and made loud music on harps and lyres. And as the ark of the covenant of the LORD came to the city of David, Michal the daughter of Saul looked out of the window, and saw King David dancing and making merry; and she despised him in her heart.*

1 Chronicles 15:28–29

There's always somebody who can't stand for anybody else to be having fun, especially in church (see Luke 15:25–28). In the earlier account of this same incident (2 Sam. 6:14–23), we are told that part of Michal's anger was at David's nakedness. Evidently she still had the problem Adam and Eve had (Gen. 3:7). We'll never know the full story of why she got so upset; she had a very neurotic father whose love of his own dignity was his downfall, and that sort of thing often gets transmitted from one generation to the next. But streaking (as David's behavior is called nowadays) is better laughed at than fussed over. Its principal fault is foolishness. And David's foolishness was in this case blessed of God.

There is a relationship between sheer human folly, and the kind of holy folly that Paul calls us to, saying, "If any one among you thinks that he is wise in this age, let him become a fool . . ." (1 Cor. 3:18) It's just about impossible to get a dignified Christian (especially a Presbyterian) to have any fun in church. This parade of David's would be as awkward to us as it was to Michal. So would Psalm 47, or Psalm 150. For that matter, so would the church in Corinth (1 Cor. 11–14) with all their shouting and carrying on. But there are some occasions, such as boys coming home from wars, or the ark from the Philistines, or that glad day when it dawns on you that your sins really are forgiven, when nothing short of dancing will do. Woe to the Presbyterians and their kin in that hour!

*O give thanks to the Lord, call on his name,*
   *make known his deeds among the peoples!*
*Sing to him, sing praises to him,*
   *tell of all his wonderful works!*
*Glory in his holy name;*
   *let the hearts of those who seek the LORD rejoice!*

David (1 Chronicles 16:8–10)

This is a continuation of the ecstatic procession dealt with on the preceding page. Now it becomes formalized. We are told that "David . . . appointed that thanksgiving be sung to the LORD by Asaph and his brethren." (1 Chron. 16:7) These songs happen to be preserved elsewhere in the Bible, in the old Hebrew Hymnbook, the Book of Psalms, 105:1–15, 96:1–13, and 106:1, 47–48. You might want to look them up and compare (the versions are slightly different). Now, this could have happened in one of several ways. Maybe David wrote the psalms for this occasion, and they became a part of the hymnbook, or else, the hymnbook was written first, and he did like we do in church, saying, "Now let's sing Hymn 105, the first three stanzas, and all of Hymn 96." Or the whole thing may have been in the mind of the Chronicler, who wrote this story in the days following the exile. He was (to judge from the difference between his work and the history in Samuel and Kings) a person very much concerned with worship, and wishing to see the ritual of the people restored to its proper place.

Which comes first, a religious experience, or a hymn? This is the same as the chicken-egg question. You have a religious experience, so you write a hymn; you sing a hymn, so you have a religious experience. All I know is, those communions who have learned to do liturgy well (like the Episcopalians) are often the best at doing spontaneous worship. That's the reason I didn't list them with the stuffy Presbyterians on the last page. Some Episcopalians have as much fun at church as Pentecostals.

## Damn my birthday!

That's not the King James Version, but that's what the Hebrew literally means. When I was a kid there used to be a Bible riddle that went:

Q. Who was the smartest baby in the Bible?

A. Job, because he cursed the day he was born. (Job 3:1) Actually Job wasn't the only one; Jeremiah did too (Jer. 20:14), and I have always been grateful to both of them. Shallow cursing, throwing *hell* and *damn* into conversations for punctuation, is worse than nonsense, but if there is a place where cursing is permissible it is in prayer. Indeed, all cursing, properly understood, is prayer, as is all blessing. To bless someone is to say, "God bless you," and "Damn you" is always short for "God damn you." God alone has either the power or the right to damn, and to invoke his condemnation lightly, or in an empty way, is to violate the third commandment. The ancient Hebrews wouldn't even speak his name at all, for fear they would use it vainly, but you don't have to speak it to violate the rule. Just as adultery is a matter of the heart as well as the body, so cursing is a sin of the soul as well as the mouth (Matt. 5:22 and 28).

But, back to praying. If there is a curse in you that has to come out, let it come out in prayer to God. His infinite grace and imperturbable eternity can absorb it. If he could handle the Devil's attack on Calvary and come out the winner, he can surely manage your puny fists beating against his gates. Have you stood beside the bed of one dying in agony who cried out, "Why, God, why?" At such a time I'm grateful for the book of Job. "Go on and cuss," I would say. "If it hurts like hell, tell God. He knows about that sort of thing." (Matt. 27:46) I don't know if my words would help anybody at such a time, but I know that Job's words have helped me in my hurting times.

*Oh that my words were written!*
*Oh that they were inscribed in a book!*
*Oh that with an iron pen and lead they were graven in the*
    *rock for ever!*
*For I know that my Redeemer lives, and at last he will*
    *stand upon the earth;*
*and after my skin has been thus destroyed, then without my*
    *flesh I shall see God, whom I shall see on my side,*
*And my eyes shall behold, and not as a stranger.*

Job 19:23–27: last four words A.S.V.

Any sentence that begins with "Oh" is a prayer of sorts, to whomever it is addressed. Here Job is crying to his three friends in particular, and to the universe in general, that, even though the evidence is to the contrary, in the end his faith in the justice of God does not waver. Read the 22 verses that precede this affirmation of faith, and see what a desperate man he is. He describes himself as diseased, alienated, and repulsive. He is barely alive, having escaped death "by the skin of my teeth." It is not the sort of man you would expect to find announcing ultimate faith in a Redeemer.

And yet, here is the high moment of the Old Testament. Unless I am mistaken, this is the only place in that venerable document in which the doctrine of the Resurrection can be found. And Job himself is not consistently sure about it; see, for instance, chapter 14. But here, in the midst of pain, anguish, and utter desolation comes a vision of vindication. It is as though one dying in ruins cries with courage: *I will not give up my belief in ultimate goodness.* Admittedly it takes another kind of courage to face the pain and ambiguities of life with heroic nihilism, or existentialist pessimism. I for one would not blame Job if he committed suicide under the circumstances. But the courage of faith is ultimately more useful than the courage of doubt, for it lends a hand to the rest of us in our struggle. The skeptic, like a sentry sleeping at his post, gains only the luxury of his own rest, and is no help to the troops. Job, boils and all, grits his teeth and helps us all hope to feel better in the morning.

*I know that thou canst do all things,*
*and that no purpose of thine can be thwarted. . . .*
*I had heard of thee by the hearing of the ear,*
    *but now my eye sees thee;*
*therefore I despise myself,*
    *and repent in dust and ashes.*

Job 42:2,5–6

At the end of the book of Job, just before the restoration of all his fortunes, comes this act of resignation. Job the curser, Job the believer, Job the self-righteous angry man, falls down in self abnegation. In a way you're kind of sorry to see him give in; what a gallant foe he was! But at last the Hound of Heaven has caught him and he knows what all people of faith come at last to know: that victory is in surrender, not in triumphal over-coming. Jesus said:

> Happiness is being meek.
> Happiness is being poor in spirit.

I take it that does *not* mean "happiness is in groveling," but in surrender. I would phrase it like this:

I am strong—not in my own strength, therefore I need not posture and pretend. My strength can be kept under control because it is the strength of God. The result is that I will not go about saying, "Aw shucks, I'm no good," rather I will live freely and joyfully as one who knows that he *is* good by the gift of Good Himself.

They say that long ago someone carved on the wall of a prison cell in the Tower of London these words:

> To serve God; to submit to fate; to undergo repentance;
> is to reign like a king.

If I understand it, this is the opposite of the old adage:

> When in danger or in doubt
> Run in circles, scream and shout.

Job's fortune is about to be restored, for he is beginning to discover that he has never lost it.

*Woe is me! For I am lost; for I am a foul-mouthed man, and I dwell in the midst of a foul-mouthed people; . . . for my eyes have seen the King, the LORD of hosts.*

Isaiah 6:5 (slightly altered after J. B. Phillips)

This is Isaiah's reaction to his vision of the Lord, high and lifted up, filling the smoky temple with his retinue, and surrounded by the singing seraphim. Our picture of angels is a little different from that of the Bible. Remember that *seraphim* and *cherubim* are plural words in Hebrew. The singular is *seraph* and *cherub*. Now what kind of picture does a *cherub* conjure up in your mind? Isn't it one of Michelangelo's fat baby angels? But the seraphim and cherubim were mighty fearsome beasts with swords and terrible voices. Almost every time they appear in the Bible they first have to say, "Don't be afraid," to the mortals who tremble at their presence (like the Bethlehem shepherds). No wonder Isaiah was scared.

You and I tend to approach God casually, as though he were an old army buddy, or a sorority sister. Where has our sense of the numinous (holy) gone? Perhaps we have begun to lose it because we have tended to substitute a kind of fake holiness for it, based on human dignity: white gloves, soft organ music, stained glass, etc. But reverence is not a matter of dignity; it's a sense of my own sinfulness.

In Isaiah's case, it took the form of feeling that he had dirty lips. (Sin in the Bible is often associated with the mouth: see for example, Psalm 12, James 3:6–12) And forgiveness comes in the form of a burning coal that makes his mouth clean (Isa. 6:6–7). Furthermore, his response (Isa. 6:8–10) is also an act of the mouth, preaching the gospel to those with stubborn ears. Perhaps there is here some justification for writing a book about prayer (matter of the heart) and spending all this time talking about (and by means of) words.

*I pray thee, LORD, is not this what I said when I was yet in my country? That is why I made haste to flee to Tarshish; for I knew that thou art a gracious God and merciful, slow to anger, and abounding in steadfast love, and repentest of evil. Therefore now, O LORD, take my life from me, I beseech thee, for it is better for me to die than to live.*

Jonah 4:2–3

"I told you so!" What delicious words in ordinary human conversation, and how astonishing to find them in a prayer! But we ought to be used, by now, to the honesty of the Hebrews. If they are angry at God, they say so. They unload their sorrows, disappointments, and indignities on him as though he were a good friend who could be trusted, or a psychiatrist who was being paid to listen. And whatever you think of Jonah, that recalcitrant prophet, you have to admit that he was always courageously honest. He admitted at once that it was he who had caused the storm that threatened his ship, and volunteered to be thrown overboard to calm the waters (1:12). Now he vents his ire at God that, because of the divine forgiveness, his doomsday warnings won't come true, his reputation as a prophet will be destroyed, and what is worse, those dreadful Ninevites won't be punished.

When you think about it, the two prayers in this little book are backward. The Psalm of deliverance (chapter 2:2–9) is really a thanksgiving, and would fit very well at the end of the book when the happy ending has taken place, while the prayer in chapter 4, with all its anger, would be very appropriate in the belly of the fish. What sort of prophet is this who sings hymns in his hour of desperation and then complains when things turn out well? Does he sound like anyone you know?

I said that Job 19 was the high point of the Old Testament. Well, maybe not. Perhaps this little book with its straightforward recognition of humanity's narrow selfishness and its vision of the God who loves all people, even the ignorant Ninevites, deserves the honors.

# V.
# SOME OF THE PSALMS

*Now there is in the Holy Scriptures a book which is distinguished from all other books of the Bible by the fact that it contains only prayers.*

*Whenever the Psalter is abandoned, an incomparable treasure vanishes from the Christian church. With its recovery will come unsuspected power.*

Dietrich Bonhoeffer, *Psalms: The Prayer Book of the Bible* (Minneapolis: Augsburg, 1970), pp. 13 and 26.

*When I look at thy heavens, the work of thy fingers,*
*the moon and the stars which thou hast established;*
*what is man that thou art mindful of him,*
*and the son of man that thou dost care for him?*
*Yet thou hast made him a little less than God,*
*and dost crown him with glory and honor.*

Psalm 8:3–5

A sense of wonder, shared by astronomers, little children, and out-door folk, is at the heart of prayer. Since the same mood is captured in the Appalachian folk carol, discovered by John Jacob Niles, it seemed good to try this song to that tune. In the process, I've also tried to include my sisters, some of whom feel left out by the language.

Why sing it at all?

1. Biblical orders (Psalm 33:3, 98:1, etc.).
2. "Whoever sings prays twice."
3. It's fun!

I wonder, as I wander out under the sky,
    How great is your name in the earth, Lord most high,
    Whose glory is heard in the little ones' cry!
I wonder, as I wander, out under the sky.

When I look at the heavens, the work of your hand,
    The moon and the stars, like the grains of the sand,
    I cannot help asking of woman and man,
    Why you should include them as part of your plan.

You've crowned them with glory as daughter and son,
    And placed them in charge of the creatures that run,
    And given them the earth for their work and their fun.
O God, how I wonder at what you have done!

*Let the words of my mouth and the meditation of my heart*
*be acceptable in thy sight,*
*O LORD, my rock and my redeemer.*

Psalm 19:14

This prayer is the concluding verse to a hymn celebrating the two silent witnesses to God: nature and law. Almost all proofs of his existence begin with one or the other:

> Ever since the creation of the world his invisible nature . . . has been clearly perceived in the things that have been made.
>
> Paul (Romans 1:20)

> First . . . human beings, all over the earth, have this curious idea that they ought to behave in a certain way.
>
> C. S. Lewis, *Mere Christianity* (N.Y.: Macmillan, 1969), p. 21.

When you put the two together like the Psalmist, it is hard to see how belief can be escaped.

If you want to sing it, try it to Jimmy Davis's song, "You Are My Sunshine."*

> The Heavens are telling God's endless glory.
> The stars and planets proclaim his worth.
> There is no language, there is no speaking;
> Yet their voice is heard in the earth.
>
> The sun arises, a shining bridegroom,
> And like a strong man, he runs his race.
> From early morning till evening shadows
> There is nothing hid from his face.
>
> God's law is perfect, the soul reviving,
> His testimony makes children wise.
> My heart rejoices in all his precepts.
> His commands enlighten my eyes.
>
> Let every thought that my mind is thinking,
> And every word that my lips unlock,
> Be in your eyesight always accepted,
> O my Redeemer and my Rock.

*For high-church folk, try Joseph Addison and Papa Haydn, "The Spacious Firmament on High."

*Lift up your heads, O gates!*
*and be lifted up, O ancient doors!*
*that the King of glory may come in.*

Psalm 24:7

Apparently a prayer can be addressed to anything, even a gate! Here the scene is readiness for a great procession, as the Lord himself enters his kingdom. It seems to me appropriate for the beginning of any worship service, but certainly for that ultimate coming in which both Old and New Testaments find hope. My tune is "When the Saints Go Marching In!" What's yours?

Chorus: Lift up your heads, you mighty gates!
Be lifted up, O ancient doors!
For the King of Glory is coming!
He will rule for ever more!

The earth is his, and all its lands,
And all the folk of every race!
For he has founded the hills and the oceans,
And put the rivers in their place!

Who shall ascend his holy hill?
Who shall stand in the place that's his?
He whose hands and heart are righteous,
And who tells it like it is!

Who is this King of which we sing?
It is the strong and mighty Lord!
Who is this King of which we are singing?
Jesus Christ, the living Word!

Chorus again.

Of course, between now and that Coming, we might also want to use this at the end of worship, singing "When the Saints Go Marching Out," to work in the world.

*When I declared not my sin, my body wasted away. . . .*
*I acknowledged my sin to thee . . .*
  *then thou didst forgive the guilt of my sin.*

Psalm 32:3, 5

Someone has said that the Psalms contain every human emotion except one: forgiveness. They are surely all there: anger, woe, desperation, love, satisfaction, and terror. And forgiveness is there too, only it is always Divine pardon. It took Jesus to tell us that to forgive is human too. Why all this emotion, sometimes even lugubrious and overblown like country music? Could it be because the Psalms *are* country music? Certainly they were written by shepherds and the like. At any rate:

> Like country music, they are overly emotional, repetitious, contradictory, earthy, angry, and full of wonder at simple things. Like *The Book of Common Prayer*, they are rich aristocratic, and moving beyond all belief. Like life itself, they are salty, sad, haunting, dancing, and worth hanging on to.*

This one makes a very suitable Declaration of Pardon for use with the prayer of confession in a worship service. My setting here is to the tune of "Michael, Row the Boat Ashore."

> Blest is he who sings this song, Alleluia!
> To whom the Lord imputes no wrong, Alleluia!
>
> When I kept a secret sin, Alleluia!
> I was deathly sick within, Alleluia!
>
> When I brought it to the day, Alleluia!
> Then the Lord took it away, Alleluia!
>
> So if you have guilt to face, Alleluia!
> God will be your hiding place, Alleluia!
>
> Praise him, every heart that lives, Alleluia!
> God in Jesus Christ forgives! Alleluia!

*McGeachy, Pat, *A New Song*, from the preface, "The Worshipbook of the Bible." (That's the first time I ever quoted from myself. Is it cheating to do that?)

*Have mercy upon me, O God, according to thy steadfast love;*
*according to thy abundant mercy blot out my transgressions.*

*Wash me thoroughly from my iniquity*
*and cleanse me from my sin!*

*For I know my transgressions,*
*and my sin is ever before me.*

*Against thee, thee only, have I sinned,*
*And done that which is evil in thy sight,*

*so that thou art justified in thy sentence*
*and blameless in thy judgment.*

*Behold, I was brought forth in iniquity,*
*and in sin did my mother conceive me.*

Psalm 51:1–5

I have printed this in couplets to emphasize the parallelism. Since the Hebrews did not know about rhyming words, they rhymed ideas! This has the happy result, as has been said, of making them translatable into any language without losing their majesty. Moreover, blank verse lends itself to prayer more readily than other styles of poetry. Even when it is rhetoric it doesn't sound like it. And the repetition is natural because heartfelt prayer invariably repeats and repeats:

> "I'm sorry, I'm sorry, I'm sorry!"
> "Holy, holy, holy!"
> "Help me! Help me!"

Here the Psalmist reiterates his guilt. In cold prose he is saying something like this:

"Forgive me, God. I know what a rat* I am. In the last analysis it was you I was rebelling against, so I deserve your anger. Even before I was born I was guilty."

A lot has been read into that last verse about the evils of sex, or about original sin, but it is simply a statement about sin's pervasiveness: we are born sinners. (Did you ever meet an unselfish baby?)

---

*Substitute your own word here.

*Create in me a clean heart, O God,*
*And put a new and right spirit within me.*

*Cast me not away from thy presence,*
*And take not thy holy Spirit from me.*

*Restore to me the joy of thy salvation,*
*And uphold me with a willing spirit.*

*O Lord, open thou my lips,*
*And my mouth shall show forth thy praise.*

*For thou hast no delight in sacrifice;*
*Were I to give a burnt offering, thou wouldst not be pleased.*

David (Psalm 51:10–12, 15–16)

What can David do to make things right again? The answer, in this case, as in the case of all sin, is absolutely nothing. There is no way he can bring back the dead Uriah. And even if there were, there is no way he can undo the disloyalty, the hurt, and the selfishness. Saying, "I won't do it again," won't help, because God knows (and David and you and I know) that he will sin again, being a man. Only by the grace of God and at his initiative can this thing be set right. Only by a miracle, which Jesus called being "born again," can a sinner get right with God.

For that reason it is no good praying a long list of righteous intentions to God, as though prayer were sort of like New Year's resolutions. For this reason, I would stay away from heroic prayers, like that of Josiah Gilbert Holland:

> *God give us men! A time like this demands strong minds, great hearts, true faith, ready hands . . . etc.*

I don't doubt that such strength is needed. It's just that I have a tendency to forget, when listing the desirable virtues, that they are fruits of the Spirit, not seeds. No amount of sacrifice on my part will do the job. Only when God creates a new heart will I become a teacher of righteousness (vs. 13), and only when he opens my mouth can I really sing!

# Give the king thy justice, O God!

Psalm 72:1

It is certainly good to pray for those in authority; in a democracy of course that means the electorate and their representatives. Moreover, as in this Psalm, prayer for social justice is at the heart of all intercession. If the Bible can use the broken relationship between man and woman as a symbol of human sin (see Hosea 1—3, Jeremiah 31:32, Ephesians 5:24, et al.), then singing about human misery is like singing a blues song. Therefore, what about putting this old plea for liberation to a song by a man who feels like giving up since his girl friend has left him? "Sometimes I get a great notion to jump in the river and drown." The tune is "Goodnight, Irene."*

> We pray for a nation of justice,
> We pray for a people in need.
> O God, make an end of oppression,
> And stamp out humanity's greed.
>
> Chorus: Praise to the Lord our God!
> Praise his glorious name!
> O may his glory fill the earth!
> Amen, I say, Amen!
>
> We pray for a prosperous nation,
> As long as the heavens endure.
> May righteousness fall like the raindrops,
> And peace on the earth be secure.
>
> We pray for the life of the nation,
> Free us from violent ways.
> O God, help the weak and the needy,
> And grant us your joy all our days.

*Again, if you're still uneasy about baptising secular tunes you may prefer Isaac Watts' setting of this Psalm. He called it "Jesus Shall Reign."

*I would rather be a doorkeeper in the house of my God
than dwell in the tents of wickedness.*

Psalm 84:10

No person lives who has not felt the longing for that true dwelling place, "a land more kind than home, more large than earth," "desire for which pierces us like a rapier at the smell of a bonfire," and "our hearts are restless" till they rest there. I suppose the Psalmist's claim is a little melodramatic, but no more so than Tom Wolfe, C. S. Lewis, and St. Augustine, all of whom I worked into that first sentence. (Sir Walter Scott is in there too if you can find him.) You just can't get too maudlin about home. That's what makes it so doubly heavy that "the Son of Man has nowhere to lay his head." (Matt. 8:20) I put this lovely Psalm to an old cowboy song about "Home on the Range."

> How lovely, O Lord, is the house of your word!
>     With my heart filled with joy I have sung!
> For the sparrow may find there a house for her kind,
>     And the swallow a nest for her young.
>
> Chorus: God's house is my home!
>     I'm happy there, singing his song.
>     I would rather keep door in the house of the Lord,
>     Than to reign in the kingdom of wrong.
>
> A day where you are is much better by far
>     Than a thousand away from your home.
> For the Lord is a light, and he keeps watch by night,
>     And his favor he gives to his own.

Almost every American can sing "Home on the Range," but there are still folk who may be reading this who don't like to sing, as hard as that is for me to handle. If so, try praying this Psalm using your own images of home: Mother, childhood, hills, house, fireside, or whatever. It is not escapism if it is your *true* home that you long for; no earthly metaphors can manage it, but they can help.

*Lord, thou hast been our dwelling place in all generations.*
*Before the mountains were brought forth, or ever thou*
*hadst formed the earth and the world,*
*from everlasting to everlasting thou art God.*
*Thou turnest man back to the dust,*
*and sayest, "Turn back, O children of men!"*
*For a thousand years in thy sight*
*are but as yesterday when it is past,*
*or as a watch in the night.*

Psalm 90:1–4

If the writer of Psalm 8 is moved by looking into the astronomical distance to a sense of wonder at God's goodness to him, this Psalmist has the opposite reaction. As he considers God's infinity and eternity, he becomes more and more conscious of his own frailty and insignificance. Listen to the words he uses to describe humanity: dust, dream, grass, sigh, toil, and trouble. And in the end he can only cry out, "O Lord, how long?"

If this is the way you are honestly feeling, then this is the way you ought to talk to God about it. (If the Psalms have a fault it is that they are so honest they make us uncomfortable in our Emersonian religion.) But bear in mind that this is not the only way to look into infinity. George Buttrick said in a memorable sermon that the miracle about Jesus was a faith that enabled him to look into that Awe-ful Abyss, and call it "Father." And Isaac Watts saw in this Psalm a hymn of comfort and hope:

> O God, our Help in ages past,
>    Our Hope for years to come,
> Be Thou our Guard while life shall last,
>    And our eternal Home.

Incidentally, next New Year's Eve you might try singing that hymn instead of "Auld Lang Syne" at your party. It nicely fits the tune and would certainly be appropriate.

*O LORD, my heart is not lifted up,*
*my eyes are not raised too high;*
*I do not occupy myself with things*
*too great and too marvelous for me.*
*But I have calmed and quieted my soul,*
*like a child quieted at its mother's breast;*
*like a child that is quieted is my soul,*
*O Israel, hope in the LORD*
*from this time forth and for evermore.*

Psalm 131

This gentle Psalm would be condemned by some as escapist, the prayer of a cop-out. But there come times when everyone must say, "I've done all I know to do , the rest I'll have to leave to God." And then lie down and go to sleep. If I were going to have my children memorize a poem to say at night I believe I would prefer this to "Now I lay me . . ." It might not be a bad thing for me to recite every evening. Indeed, it is hard for me to read it over without feeling more relaxed. It is a song of trust.

Here's a further trick, perfected with the Geneva and Scottish Psalters during the Reformation, that you can play with the Psalms: rewrite them to fit unfamiliar tunes. Here we tread again dangerously near the doggerel line, but it gives us the added advantage of easy remembering and the emotional content of the music. For Psalm 131 I have chosen the oldest lullaby I remember, "Rockabye Baby," since it is a quiet, comforting, familiar melody:

O Lord, my heart is not lifted up.
My eyes are not raised upward too high.
I do not worry myself with things
Too marvelous and too great for me.

But I have calmed and quieted my soul,
Like a child quiet at his mother's breast.
A child that is quieted, is my soul,
From this time forth and forever more.

Note that I have left out the injunction to Israel in the last verse, because here, I believe, the Psalmist had quit praying and gone to preaching.

*Praise the LORD from the earth,*
  *you sea monsters and all deeps,*
*fire and hail, snow and frost,*
  *stormy wind fulfilling his command!*
*Mountains and all hills, fruit trees and all cedars!*
*Beasts and all cattle, creeping things and flying birds!*
*Kings of the earth and all peoples,*
  *princes and all rulers of the earth!*
*Young men and maidens together, old men and children!*
*Let them praise the name of the LORD!*

Psalm 148:7–11

How do you picture every single thing in the universe joining in a grand Hallelujah? C. S. Lewis called it "the great dance," and you may enjoy his fantastic description of it in the last chapter of *Perelandra*. Psalm 98 hears the waves clapping their hands. Isaac Watts interpreted that psalm like this:

> Joy to the world! The Saviour reigns:
> Let men their songs employ;
> While fields and floods, rocks, hills, and plains,
> Repeat the sounding joy.

The image that I have is that of a round, voices coming from the four corners of the earth. (My tune is Row, Row, Row.)

> Praise God in the heights! Praise him on the earth!
> Praise, praise, praise, praise! Praise for all you're worth!
>
> Praise him, sun and moon! Praise him shining stars!
> Hills, trees, creeping things, trains and planes and cars!
>
> Praise him, all the earth; monsters of the deep!
> Fire, hail, frost, snow! Waking or asleep!
>
> Praise him, presidents, judges, congressmen!
> Girls, women, men, boys! Praise him once again!

But whether you can buy into that image or not, can you picture yourself praising God with what you do: driving nails, washing dishes, making rounds, doing homework, pushing buttons. If so, your whole life is a prayer. If not, have you considered getting into some other line of work?

# VI.
## NEW TESTAMENT PRAYERS

*If I pray in a tongue, my spirit prays, but my mind is unfruitful. What am I to do? I will pray with the spirit and I will pray with the mind also; I will sing with the spirit and I will sing with the mind also. Otherwise, if you give thanks to God with the spirit, how can any one . . . say the "Amen" to your thanksgiving when he does not know what you are saying?*

1 Corinthians 14:14–16

*We do not know how to pray as we ought, but the Spirit himself intercedes for us with sighs too deep for words.*

Romans 8:26

*Lord, if you will, you can make me clean.*

A Leper (Matthew 8:2)

I suppose that prayer for healing is the most common of our intercessions. The one place in many Protestant worship services where the whole congregation gets involved in the praying is in the "pastoral" prayer at this point. Some prayer books call for stopping here to let the people on board with their concerns about loved ones and friends. One reads like this:

> *Show thy loving-kindness unto all men and women and little children, according to the need of every living soul, especially unto those whom we love, and those who are in any kind of trouble or distress, whom we now remember silently before thee (here let there be a moment of prayer in silence).*

In less formal services the leader may ask the congregation to name aloud the sick among them, or the attention of the Lord will be called to the announcement page of the bulletin where they are listed. Pastors make more prayers in hospitals than in any other place outside their church buildings. Does it do any good?

The leper who spoke the prayer at the top of this page obviously thought that the Lord had the power to heal. Would he do it? Yes, if he chose to. But why does he not *always* choose to? Doesn't he know our needs already (Matt. 6:8, 32), and isn't he concerned about every falling bird (Matt. 10:29)? Well yes, certainly. It is never his will that any of his little ones should perish (Matt. 18:14). But it is clear (Matt. 10:28) that the destruction of the body is not what "perishing" is all about. One can live fat and well in body, and be shriveled and dead in soul. And even fatal disease is not inevitably the conqueror. To pray for *healing* is to pray for wholeness. Indeed there is a whole family of related words descending from a common Old Teutonic root: *heal, hale, whole, hail, Hello* (health to you) and the German word for salvation: *das Seelenheil.* It is not an accident that the word *salve*, meaning a healing ointment, is related to the word *salvation.* To pray for healing is to expect the body to get well, yes, but it is also to ask for much more than that.

*Lord, if it is you, bid me come to you on the water.*

Peter (Matthew 14:28)

I don't know how many dumb things Peter said to Jesus in their few years together. Things like: " 'God forbid, Lord! This shall never happen to you,' " (Matt. 16:22) which prompted Jesus to call him Satan, or like, " 'I will not deny you,' " (Matt. 26:35). But I am grateful for all of them. If Peter says dumb things, then maybe there is hope for me that I will someday say the right things the way Peter did eventually: (such as Matt. 16:16 or Acts 4:7–12). Besides, most of his errors in judgment, were, like this one, based on an over-abundance of optimism, and you have to like him for his enthusiasm at any rate. But this prayer is especially problematic. In the first place it is putting Jesus to the test, which is against the rules (Matt. 4:7). This is done many times in the Bible, from Gideon's putting out the fleece (Judges 6:36–40), to the casting of lots to decide on a replacement for Judas (Acts 1:15–26), but always with a kind of uneasiness ("Let not thy anger burn against me.") In the second place, it is asking for a kind of special treatment (much like the ambitious Mrs. Zebbedee: Matt. 20:20–28), and thirdly, it ill becomes a person to try to walk on water before he has learned to walk well on the earth.

Back in the thirties, the Ford Motor Company sponsored a nation-wide tour of a giant, mechanically-operated map of the Holy Land, with miniature cities, and moving characters illustrating Bible stories. I remember staring in fascination at the animated Jesus lifting his arms and raising drowning Peter from the water. Then, as I watched, Jesus would lower his arms and Peter would be dunked again. Over and over the little man was "sinking deep in sin" and then lifted again by love. That is sort of the story of Peter's life and mine, and the way of my prayers: I ask for and commit myself to more than I can handle, then I fall on my face, and ask again. Will the day ever come when I can pray for what I really need, and be satisfied with that, or must I ever bite off more than I can chew?

## *I believe; help my unbelief!*

A worried father (Mark 9:24)

This is an honest prayer, the more remarkable because it was spoken under conditions when a lie would have been very tempting. His son is possessed of a demon (epilepsy?), and Jesus has just promised him that cure is possible, saying, "All things are possible to him who believes." At that point, whatever the father felt, for the sake of the boy he must have been tempted to say, "Yes, I believe; cure him!" And part of him did say that. But there is something about Jesus' presence that makes a lie tear us like a vomit; it won't do. So the skeptical half of the man pours out its admission of doubt.

Will I lose it all if I admit to God in my prayers that I don't like what he wants me to do, that I haven't done what I knew he wanted me to, or that some days I'm not even sure if I believe in him at all? No, I *will* lose it all, though, if I build a religious life on pretense and empty phrases. God knows whether I believe or not; I'd better know it myself.

I have been thinking of some prayers that aren't very religious, but are at least attempts at the truth:

> *O God, if there be a God . . .*
> *My God, my God, why hast thou forsaken me!*
> *Lord I don't know if you are listening. My words seem to bounce back to me off the ceiling . . .*

No form of prayer is more likely to "work" than pure and untarnished honesty. Even if my feeling is one of open hostility toward God (Job 3:1–10), it is better to speak it aloud than to coat it with sugary phrases. A lie unconfessed is like a tumor undetected: until the surgeon's knife cuts it out, it festers, and one day dooms. But one who makes open war on God at least has the hope that he may be overrun by him and conquered. This happened to Paul on the Damascus road, and to this weeping father, whose unbelief was confessed and overcome.

*My soul magnifies the Lord,*
 *and my spirit rejoices in God my Savior,*
 *for he has regarded the low estate of his handmaiden.*
*For behold, henceforth all generations will call me blessed;*
 *for he who is mighty has done great things for me,*
 *and holy is his name.*

Mary (Luke 1:46–49)

This lovely hymn, only part of which is given here, was prayed by Mary after hearing a prophecy from her cousin Elizabeth concerning the forthcoming birth of her son. It is doubtful that this prayer (like the other hymns in the first two chapters of Luke) was created spontaneously in the act of conversation. Indeed, this particular one (which is sometimes called *The Magnificat*, after the Latin word with which it begins) is found in another version on the lips of our old friend Hannah, way back in 1 Samuel 2:1–10. (See page 47 of this book.)

Can you use a formal prayer or traditional hymn as a personal prayer? Well sure! See Jesus' use of the Psalms during his crucifixion (pages 96–99). I can think of a number of instances in which I have quoted hymns as acts of personal prayer. Especially true is this of first lines (which is all I can remember of a lot of hymns). I can hear myself saying, under certain conditions:

"Take my life, and let it be consecrated . . ."

or "Just as I am, I come . . ."

or "O God, Abide with me!"

Once during a particularly dull church meeting I found myself singing with heavy monotony:

"Like a mighty army, moves the Church of God . . ." But I confess that I did that more for the benefit of the audience around me than an expression of faith. It's pretty dangerous to use sarcasm in prayer. (Not illegal though; God is very fond of sarcasm: see Amos 4:4–5, or Matthew 7:3–5.) Sometimes when you find out you are pregnant, or you have just gotten a book published, or school is over for the summer, a hymn is very much in order.

*To you I will give all this authority and their glory; for it has been delivered to me, and I give it to whom I will. If you, then, will worship me, it shall all be yours.*

Satan (Luke 4:6)

Does the Devil ever pray? Well, of course, if he talks to Jesus. All conversation with God is prayer. Frankly, I have problems with the Devil as a person, since if he is all evil he must be irrational, and thus not a person. And I don't see how you can claim that there's any good in him. But I know for sure that the Devil gets into all of us, and the Devil in us prays. See, for example, in that same chapter in Luke, the cry of the demon to Jesus (4:34). But demons don't cry out unless they know they are about to be cast out; it is their last extremity. Usually they keep silent lest they be discovered for what they are. As long as we keep on referring to certain drives in ourselves as "natural feelings," or "neuroses," or "super ego," we will coddle them. Only when we can call them demonic can we really get a feel for their insidious nature, and learn to attack them frontally. The phrase may be medieval, but it has power.

Note that the Devil's prayer is basically this: "God, worship me!" That, in the end, is where all false prayer leads. George Macdonald said, "The one principle of Hell is, "I am my own.' "* It may be right to confess honestly to God that I want *my* will to be done, but until I can come to terms with my need for his will to be done, I am still struggling with the dark against the light. I used to think that Hell (in the spiritual sense) meant separation from God. In a way, of course, it does. But in another sense it can never be that. There is no way to get away from God (Ps. 139:8). Heaven is being in the presence of God, having at last learned to carry a tune, and singing his praises with joy (Rev. 4:8). But Hell is being in the presence of God, hating the sound of hymns, and gibbering over and over again, "Stop that awful noise!"

*C. S. Lewis, *George Macdonald: An Anthology.*

*Are you he who is to come, or shall we look for another?*

John the Baptist (Luke 7:19)

This is the prayer of a man who is skirting the edges of doubt. He has already affirmed his faith in Jesus, now he is beginning to wonder. Thousands of new Chritians have known similar feelings. I have been moved to put my trust in the Lord, and at first life seemed radically new and different; now things are falling back into the old patterns. The world isn't any better. I'm still guilty of my old sins: short temper, over-indulgence. I'm still living with the same cross-patch of a mate, and don't seem to be able to stand it with Christian patience. "Lord, are you really in charge of my life? If so, why aren't things different?"

Jesus' answer to John was this: "Look around you. The blind receive their sight, the lame walk, lepers are cleansed, and the deaf hear, the dead are raised up, the poor have good news preached to them."* He didn't say yes or no. In fact, Jesus rarely answers that way. (See, for instance, Matt. 22:15–22, 27:11, John 18:33–34). I suppose that God, if he chose, could rearrange the stars in heaven to spell out "I AM GOD, BELIVE IN ME." If he did, there would still be some of us who would not believe (Luke 16:31) and those who did believe would do so, not out of faith and devotion, but out of necessity. And one who obeys out of necessity is a slave, not a son. He wants us to be his children. So he leaves unanswered our question. At any rate he will not give us the obvious answer. But in our hearts of hearts, if we look at the world we do know that wherever Christ's love is put to work, it is a better place. No, it isn't perfect yet. For a resort hotel, it stinks. But for the battlefield it is, it's not so bad.

---

*Why do you suppose, in this quote from Isaiah, Jesus left out the part about people in prison? He was addressing a man in jail. Jesus often purposefully omitted things. (See page 90, concerning the rich young man and the law.)

*Father, I have sinned against heaven and before you; I am no longer worthy to be called your son.*

The Prodigal (Luke 15:18)

This prayer was prayed in a pigpen. That's a bad enough place for anybody to be, but remember that this was a good Jewish boy, which made it even worse. He had blown his last dime on bad liquor and bad women. It may be hard to pray in a pigpen, but what is even harder is to pray when you know you have been a bad boy. What keeps most of us from praying is not that we don't know the right words, or how to use them, but that we are ashamed to talk to God. We have ignored him for so long that we doubt if he would listen. Or, what's worse, we're afraid that he will. And what's still worse, that he will speak, and give us new and terrible orders which we will never be able to carry out, and it will all ends up a hell of a mess. (I suppose in the theological sense what I really mean is a mess of a hell.) That is the fear we have, and it keeps us from praying. We feel too silly (especially those of us who have been taught to be tough-minded, self-made, independent, rugged individualists, or competent executives), or too guilty.

But please note what happened when this miserable boy finally got around to being straight with his father. Instead of making him a servant, they gave him the robe and ring, symbols of sonship, killed the best beef they had waiting, hired musicians, and threw a party. What do you think would happen if you and I opened up ?

*Lo, these many years I have served you, and I never dis-
obeyed your command; yet you never gave me a kid, that
I might make merry with my friends. But when this son of
yours came, who has devoured your living with harlots,
you killed for him the fatted calf!*

The Older Son (Luke 15:29–30)


If it is hard to pray in a pigsty, it is even harder to pray in a palace. But if
the best you can do is gripe about how unfair the world is when sinners are saved
by grace, and those of us who have kept the rules get left out of the fun, then
by all means pray that. If you think you deserved a party and a fatted calf too,
you are wrong. But you could always have asked for one. You can ask for one now.
Come on, join the dance, you stuffed shirt!

*God, be merciful to me a sinner.*

A tax collecter (Luke 18:13)

This is the prayer of a kind of Palestinian quisling, who had sold out to the conqueror Romans, who prayed at one end of the temple, while a Pharisee (a member of the leading religious party of Jerusalem, whose WASP equivalent would be a member of Downtown First Church) prayed at the other. The Pharisee's prayer was full of self-satisfaction:

> *"God, I thank thee that I am not like other men, extortioners, unjust, adulterers, or even like this tax collector. I fast twice a week, I give tithes of all that I get."*

But Jesus gives his stamp of approval to the prayer of the social outcast. What was there about it that made him justified?

It wasn't his posture. (He just stood there—didn't even kneel.)

It wasn't whether his eyes were shut or not. (He wouldn't even look at God. Maybe we make far too much over this deal; try praying with your eyes fixed on some object to guide your prayer: a window, a passage of Scripture, a banner, a face.)

It wasn't his eloquence. (He loses the word contest with the Pharisee, 33 to 7.)

It wasn't his dignity. (He pounded on his chest like an ape.)

It was, Jesus tells us (vs. 14), his humility.

This scripture troubles me. It troubles me because of a subtle catch to it. Every time I think I have got its message and discovered the meaning of humility, I catch myself praying:

> *God, I thank thee that my prayers are not long-winded, or self-centered, or pious, or eloquent, or pompous, or even like this Pharisee. I pray like a person of flesh and blood who means in all humility what he says.*

About the time I get like that something saves me, like when my son Martin, on his first trip to church, punched his mother and asked, "When we get back home, will Daddy talk like he really does?"

*Lord Jesus, receive my spirit. Lord, do not hold this sin against them.*

Stephen (Acts 7:59, 60)

These are the last words of Stephen, echoing the last words of Jesus: "Father into thy hands I commit my spirit," and "Father, forgive them, for they know not what they do." I don't think I would have the courage to pray the first or the humility to pray the second. Not while being stoned to death, at any rate.

But I don't know about that. I have never been stoned to death, so I can't tell you how I would react under the circumstances. Most people have more courage than they give themselves credit for having. All young men going into battle wonder if they will be able to carry it off with honor, and most of them do.

With me, I know that little things tend to upset me more than big things. Coat-hangers tangled in closets, rude drivers, inefficient sales-persons—that sort of thing will set my temper off or put me in a depressed mood. But when I have to face the death of loved ones, or great sorrow with my children, somehow my strength surprises me. So I'd like to hope that I would be faithful before the firing squad.

But the trouble with all that is that I probably won't be called upon to face a firing squad. Martyrs are rare, and you don't get to chose the cause you die for anyway. You have to stand your ground on little things: a nasty racial slur by your barber, or a question of honesty on your income tax. When those moments come, then may God give us all the grace to stand faithful.

"When Stephen, full of power and grace . . ."

(Look up that hymn in *The Worshipbook,* page 638.)

*For this reason I bow my knees before the Father, from whom every family in heaven and on earth is named, that according to the riches of his glory he may grant you to be strengthened with might through his Spirit in the inner man, and that Christ may dwell in your hearts through faith; that you, being rooted and grounded in love, may have power to comprehend with all the saints what is the breadth and length and height and depth, and to know the love of Christ which surpasses knowledge, that you may be filled with all the fulness of God.*

Paul (Ephesians 3:14–19)

This is a prayer of St. Paul, although strictly speaking it is his *description* of a prayer. What he actually says to God we leave to the privacy of his meditations; this is an explanation to his readers of what he is praying about on their behalf. Here we have a good suggestion to all public pray-ers, clerical or lay. Instead of praying aloud, and allowing the congregation to listen in, what if we explained to the people what we're going to say to God, and why, and then let all pray silently? That would certainly eliminate any tendency to preach in the prayer itself. It could go something like this:

> Christian friends, I am going to ask God to give us healing, for I know that there are many sick among us, and that even those who are well need his protection from disease and disability. I'm thinking this morning of ————, and ————, and ————, who are in the hospital. Please tell me the names of others that you want to include.

Then, after a time of sharing there might be silence, or the leader might simply say:

> *O God, you've heard our talk, and the names we have named. You know our hurt, and how badly we need your help. Please give us healing, through Jesus Christ our Lord.*

Is that an audacious thing to ask? Certainly not more audacious than Paul's prayer that we be filled with all the fulness of God. There is no greater miracle than that of putting eternity into a finite container.

*Amen! Blessing and glory and wisdom and thanksgiving and honor and power and might be to our God for ever and ever! Amen.*

The Assembly in the Throne Room (Revelation 7:12)

There are two ways of looking at it. You can either say that when we get to heaven we won't have to go to church at all (see Rev. 21:22) or that in heaven all you do is go to church. Either way adds up to the same thing: those who love to praise God get their reward; those who love to curse him get theirs. If the old catechism is right, and the chief end of man is to "glorify God and enjoy him forever" then it is very logical that eternity be spent in singing hymns.

Now let's not misunderstand each other. I don't pretend that I, or even the writer of The Revelation, really know what things will be like in heaven. "No eye has seen, nor ear heard, nor the heart of man conceived, what God has prepared for those who love him." (1 Cor. 2:9) I have some ways of thinking about it that are useful for me, but they would probably not be very helpful to you because the only language we can use is that of poetry, which expresses truths that the words of science and everyday conversation can't handle, but which has to be very personal. For instance, the images of golden streets, pearly gates, and gem-encrusted buildings (Rev. 21:19–21) do not help me very much, since I do not care particularly for jewelry. But the description of the river, and the tree of life, its leaves for the healing of the nations (Rev. 22:1–2) is very moving to me, since I am a nature-lover.

But singing (while it may not appeal to everybody) is a pretty universal way of expressing some of our emotions, and I, who love to sing, can picture myself singing the bass in the heavenly choir which no man can number. ( I even have to watch out not to sing too loud!) Of course not many of us would want to play the harp forever and ever and ever. But if harp playing is a Bible metaphor for doing that which your heart of hearts has truly desired above all things, and of which every earthly desire is only a copy, then indeed heaven is something to look forward to.

# VII.
## PRAYERS OF JESUS

*When you pray, you must not be like the hypocrites; for they love to stand and pray in the synagogues and at the street corners, that they may be seen by men. Truly, I say to you, they have received their reward. But when you pray, go into your room and shut the door and pray to your Father who is in secret. . . .*

*And in praying do not heap up empty phrases as the Gentiles do; for they think that they will be heard for their many words. Do not be like them, for your Father knows what you need before you ask him.*

*Pray then like this. . . .*

Matthew 6:5–8

*Our Father in heaven.*

"Pray then, like this," said Jesus, and proceeded to give an example. I doubt if he intended for it to be repeated Sunday after Sunday in exactly the same form, and I'm certain he never wanted it to become a repetitious sing-song chant. (Did you know that the English word *patter* comes from the opening words of this prayer in Latin: *pater nostrum?* Worse than that, the word *hocus-pocus* is is a corruption of the words of the consecration at the Communion: *hic est corpus;* "this is the body!") The language used here is that of the International Consultation on English in the Liturgy. But of course, Jesus originally spoke the prayer in his language, Aramaic, and the opening word may have been *Abba* (see Mark 14:36, Romans 8:15). It was Jesus who enabled us at last to look into the dreadful abyss of Eternity, on which man cannot look and live (Exod. 33:20), and address that infinity with the most intimate word of childhood.

If you are female, please know that though the Hebrew language is very paternalistic, the Bible is clear that God is both masculine and feminine. "Male and female" we are his image (Gen. 1:27). "As a father pities his children, so the LORD pities those who fear him" (Ps. 103:13), yes, but see also Isaiah 66:13: "As one whom his mother comforts, so I will comfort you." And of course the New Testament seals it with Paul's words, "There is neither male nor female; for you are all one in Christ Jesus." (Gal. 3:28) I sometimes wonder if one of the reasons that Jesus and Paul did not marry was to prevent them from having to act out the traditionally masculine role of the Hebrew husband, so that they could be "all things to all men (persons)." But no matter. The important thing is that the expression is one of childhood's innocent intimacy. I think the Tshiluba (Zairian) word for mother is *Baba,* which is pretty close to *Abba;* I wonder if there is any primordial etymological connection.

The words "in heaven" make it clear that we are not talking about an ordinary earthly parent; they are part of his title, as we recognize when we sometimes say it the other way around as small children do: "Hemly Fadda." They know something.

*Holy be your name.*

Matthew 6:9

Of course God's name is already holy. We don't make it so by uttering these words, any more than our pleas for mercy turn God's wrath into smiles by changing his mind. The change that takes place is in us. When we proclaim his holiness, it becomes a reality for us. When we beg for his mercy, it happens that we suddenly discover that he is merciful. Thus, the Kyrie with which the Mass begins can appropriately be rendered either penitentially: "Lord have mercy upon us," or as a joyful affirmation of faith, "You are the Lord, giver of mercy!"

To acknowledge God's holiness is at once both a positive and a negative experience. One reaction is, "Woe is me! I am a dirty-mouthed man!" (Isa. 6:5) And the other is joyful and loyal obedience to the Holy One, as though I have sought nothing else all my life. "Here I am! Send me!" (Isa. 6:8) Thus, when he encounters Pan on his island, the Rat cries, his eyes shining with unutterable love, " 'Afraid! Of *Him?* O, never, never! And yet—and yet O, Mole, I am afraid!' "*

Holy means set apart, separated, removed. So when Jesus calls God by the intimate term, "Father," he has not eliminated reverence as a proper attitude for the Christian. But reverence is not the same as stuffiness! You might think it is, judging from some of our worship services, conducted like funerals, with somber organ dirges and boutonniered lapels. Maybe that is why we are uncomfortable when the International Text says "your name" instead of "Thy name." That is strange, too, since grammatically, *your* is the formal pronoun, and *Thy* is the familiar form, still thus used among some of the Friends' meetings. But it doesn't matter which pronoun you use, provided you remember that you are speaking to a real Person, who hears and answers.

I'm not ready yet to suggest a substitute for the old word "reverence," but I'll admit I warm to an expression I heard from a visitor in a very informal church. He was used to a rather stiff worship service, and at first all the informality bothered him. But at length it dawned on him that something good was happening here. "You know," he said, "I like this casual reverence." I do too.

---

*Kenneth Grahame, *The Wind in the Willows* (N.Y.: Charles Scribner's Sons, 1964), p. 136.

*Your kingdom come.*

Matthew 6:10

No phrase more dangerous has been repeated more glibly. It was popular among the young during the forties to say, "Drop dead!" But what would we have felt if the person to whom we were speaking had suddenly keeled over? And what an astonishment to the thousands of Christians on Sunday morning, mouthing the Lord's Prayer with their minds on other things, if it suddenly happened. What would it be like? Different folk have different visions of the kingdom of God. "You won't like it," said Amos the prophet (5:18–20). "It is darkness and not light; as if you thought you were escaping from a lion, and a bear got you; or finally getting to the security of your home and there you were bit by a snake." (author's paraphrase) However, that is for the evil folk of the world, wrote Malachi (4:1–2), "but for you who fear my name the sun of righteousness shall rise, with healing in its wings."

The question is, who are the evil guys and who are the good guys. Of course the good are members of my church. Oh? Well, then members of some church. Really? The Bible says that in heaven there aren't any church-goers (Rev. 21:22). And all those thousands of jokes you have heard about St. Peter guarding the gates of heaven and letting in the worthy are lies. Those gates are never closed! (Rev. 21:25) Of course nothing evil or filthy can get in (21:27), but that is not because they are not good enough. *Nobody* is good enough. Those who get in do so because of the grace of God. This means really that those who love God will find him (Matt. 5:3–11), and those who hate God will find what *they* love (Matt. 6:2, 5, and 16). If we put our trust in earthly power and pleasure, that is what we will get, and in it we will die. But if we really seek obedience to the King, then in the King's service we will live.

Go ahead and pray it, but don't be surprised if it actually does come.

*Your will be done, on earth as it is in heaven.*

Matthew 6:10

At this point I sort of wish I had a copy of Dr. Watershed's book, *How to Know God's Will,* if there is one. I could use some counsel. Why, if God is almighty, isn't his will already being done on earth? This petition seems to be saying that there is an ideal sense (and an ideal place) in which God's will *is* being done, that his kingdom *has* come. This was the conviction of the early Christians in their basic creed: "Jesus is Lord!" (1 Cor. 12:3) But it certainly isn't being done as I look at the world around me. All I need is one miscarriage, one starving Biafran baby, one alcoholic suicide, one destructive marriage, one murder, or even one drowned baby duck to convince me of this. "It is not the will of my Father who is in heaven that one of these little ones should perish." (Matt. 18:14, at the conclusion of the Parable of the Lost Sheep) If Jesus is really Lord, why is this so?

Well, in one sense it is absurd for me to ask "why" about anything concerning God. I might just as helpfully ask, "Why, if there is no God, is there a universal conviction among man that we ought to be good?" The problem of good is at least as knotty as the problem of evil. And I doubt if I can solve it when Augustine and Calvin and Barth and Tillich haven't managed it yet. But I can turn it over in my head, and so can you. When I do, it comes out like this: The only stories worth reading are those in which the hero has a battle on his hands. *Superman* is no fun unless you invent some green kryptonite to render him weak enough to be in trouble. Oak trees grow strong in the soil of adversity. Only out of freedom comes responsibility, and only in dying can we be born again to eternal life.

If God wills for you and me a struggle that will make us strong, then his will is certainly being done. And if I want to be strong, then I should pray: "Your will be done." *Que sera, sera* anyway. (Well, do you believe what will be *won't* be?)

*Give us today our daily bread.*

Matthew 6:11

As in our time, the word *bread* here means more than food. This is a request for all the necessities of life. And that raises the question: What is it proper for me to pray for? Would it be appropriate to ask God to give me a diamond pendant? If one should pray for necessities, dare one pray for luxuries? But what is a luxury? It depends on what your god is. There was a certain young man (Mark 10:17–22) whose possessions kept him from obeying. He asked Jesus, "What must I do to inherit eternal life?" and the Lord responded by listing some of the commandments, which the youth claimed to have kept since childhood. I suspect he had, for he was a fellow of remarkable dedication. But note that Jesus left out the first three commandments, having to do with the worship of God, and the last, which has to do with covetousness. He knew that money was a god for the young man, and that until he exorcised that false sovereign, he could not follow the true source of happiness.

Now there is somewhere in this world a budding genius at the violin who might well pray for a Stradivarius, or a potential physician who should ask for the "bread" to provide a medical education. But for most of us, what we really need is warm clothes, nutritional food, and good friends. Beyond that, who cares? It is more fun to expect surprises than to demand them of God. Anyway, whatever we pray for, he's going to give us what we need. "If you, mean as you are, know how to give good gifts to your children, how much more will your Father who is in heaven give good things to those who ask him!" (Matt. 7:11, author's paraphrase of Edgar J. Goodspeed) If we pray for bread we know he will not give us a stone; and if, conversely, we make the mistake of praying for a stone, believing it really is a diamond pendant that we must have, he will give us our daily bread. He knows we can't eat rocks.

Then why pray at all, you ask? More about that on the next two pages.

*Forgive us our sins as we forgive those who sin against us.*

Why do we need to pray for forgiveness? Has not God already forgiven us, and did he not already seal that in the death of Jesus long ago? Well yes, and blessed is the one who knows that, because true happiness starts there. But we still ask for it, as we ask for our daily bread, because there is no forgiveness for one who does not think he needs it. The one unforgiveable sin is the sin that will not be admitted: that is to claim that one's evil deeds are in fact good. For the Pharisees (Matt. 12:22–33) this took the form of blaspheming against the Holy Spirit. They called a good work by Jesus the work of the Devil. But their own legalism they saw as true good. For such sins there is no forgiveness. Not because God is vindictive, but because forgiveness is a gift, and a gift can only be of use to one who has the humility to accept it. As long as we get the sulks, like spoiled children, and say, "I don't wanna go to the nasty old circus anyway," we'll never get to see the clowns. And as long as we shout, "You know what you can do with your bleeding charity!" we are lost in our prison of self-sufficiency. But the poor soul who wonders if his sins are forgiven has not yet committed the unpardonable one. He is still willing to face the truth.

Jesus gives us a clue to our openness to forgiveness by adding these words (Matt. 6:14–15) after the prayer:

> For if you forgive men their trespasses, your heavenly Father also will forgive you; but if you do not forgive men their trespasses, neither will your Father forgive your trespasses.

Again, it is not that God is keeping score, but that the heart which cannot give forgiveness is incapable of receiving it. The one sure road to hell is: "I demand my rights!" Make that kind of statement at the "pearly gates" and you can expect a one way ticket to the palace where *your* will will be done. In heaven you get to do God's will, and if you don't dig that, then that's the hell of it.

It might help to rephrase this petition: "Lord, help me to forgive those around me, so that I can learn to accept forgiveness from you."

*Do not bring us to the test but deliver us from evil.*

Matthew 6:13

Seen from the human point of view this looks a little like we suspect God of deliberately tormenting and teasing us with the possibility that we may fall, in which case, I suppose we would hear the Divine Raspberry: "Nyah, nyah, nyah!" (See Psalm 2:4.) But that view is childish and itself deserves derision (see James 1:13). Nobody who looks Jesus honestly in the face can see in him one who would deliberately tempt us and try to trip us up (see John 17:15). So we'll have to try to see it from the perspective of the parent, not the child. From that direction it looks as though Jesus, knowing that we are going to encounter really tough moral issues, is encouraging us to pray for the strength to escape them. Through the repetition of this prayer, as a weight-lifter builds up his muscles, we build up our resistance to temptation.

Besides that, if we are honest, we don't want to have to face such treacherous ground, and Jesus knows this, so he puts in this phrase as an honest expression of our fears. This is our version of "Father, if it be possible, let this cup pass from me." And we conclude it, saying, "But if it has to be, help me make it through." Perhaps the phrase would take on fresh meaning if it were phrased something like this: "God, I'm scared I'll fail you, don't let me do it."

Furthermore, this petition is an admission that all our righteousness comes from God, not from ourselves. For that matter, even our prayer comes from God. There is a sense in which all prayer is God talking to himself. It is the Father who moves me to pray, his Son who gives me the example, and his Spirit who intercedes for me below the level of the verbal. In that case, why should I bother to pray at all, especially since God knows my need before I ask him? (Matt. 6:32) Well simply because the great dance of life is going on and I don't want to sit it out. To refuse to play my part in the divine conversation is to miss the main point of life: to glorify and enjoy God.

*For the kingdom, the power, and the glory are yours now and forever.*

This closing doxology was not part of Jesus' original prayer, as it is not in the earliest manuscripts, but it was added very soon by the early church, and rightly so, for it is fitting that the prayer end as it began: with praise to God. The whole tone of the Lord's prayer is one of great humility. In praying it, we are affirming that God is heavenly, not earthly, that he, not we, is holy, that it is his kingdom and his will that we seek, that he is the giver of daily strength, that only with his help can we escape temptation. So it is with a ringing affirmation of that perspective that the traditional form of this prayer ends. (Luke's version in 11:2–4 is even shorter than Matthew's.)

What a liberating thing this prayer is! It never says, "I'll try harder." It never says, "I'll do my best." It lays no demands on me, it leaves it all up to God, up to and including my own morality. It is not so presumptuous as St. Francis who asks God to "make me an instrument." Compared to it, even Reinhold Niebuhr's famous prayer for serenity:

> *God grant me the serenity to accept the things I cannot change, the courage to change the things I can, and the wisdom to know the difference*

has a touch of arrogance to it. Jesus' model seems to be saying rather: "God, change things, for yours is the power." Is this then a cop-out? Do we leave it all up to God and go lie down and suck our theological and ethical thumbs? In actual practice it doesn't seem to work out that way. Whenever the human race, or the Church, or an individual becomes freshly aware of the free gift of God's grace, and the realization that nothing we can do will bring in the kingdom, the result is fresh activity. When Luther and Calvin reintroduced the doctrine of "justification by faith," the Reformation burst forth. When a child learns that his parents hurt with him (not against him) for his bad report cards, his grades start improving. To have guilt removed is to become free for joyful service.

*Father, the hour has come; glorify thy Son, that the Son may glorify thee.*

*I have manifested thy name to the [disciples] whom thou gavest me out of the world. . . . I am praying for them.*

*As thou didst send me into the world, so I have sent them into the world.*

*I do not pray for these only, but also for those who are to believe in me through their word, that they may all be one; even as thou, Father, art in me, and I in thee, that they also may be in us, so that the world may believe that thou hast sent me.*

John 17:1–26 (excerpts)

This is the great prayer of Jesus in the upper room. It is the longest recorded prayer of his that we have. (Not the longest that he prayed, however, for more than once he prayed all night. And not the longest prayer in the Bible; see, for example, Solomon's liturgical longevity in 1 Kings 8, or 2 Chronicles 9.) But that isn't important. We even find him violating my rule by explaining things to God (see verse 3), or to the disciples. That isn't very important either. Funny thing, Jesus is forever breaking people's rules. You can't pin him down.

> He will always prove the most elusive of teachers. Systems cannot keep up with that darting illumination. No net less wide than a man's whole heart, nor less fine of mesh than love, will hold the sacred Fish.*

What is important is what this prayer teaches about the nature of God. It is a hymn to unity. He will not take his disciples out of the world; rather he sends us into the world, in, but not of it, to bear the pain of its brokenness, till the unity that God wills shall come to pass. (See Ephesians 1:9–10 and 2:11–22) He who prays to that God, through this Jesus, can expect to give up all griefs except that.

---

*C. S. Lewis, *Reflections on the Psalms*, (N.Y.: Harcourt, Brace, and World, 1958), p. 119.

*My Father, if it be possible, let this cup pass from me;*
*nevertheless, not as I will, but as thou wilt.*

Three times Jesus said this, apparently both wishing the burden to go away, and disciplining himself to bear it. For this prayer, as for his cry of desolation from the cross, I give most grateful thanks, for it is here that Jesus lets me know that he understands my humanity. When I meet him cooly dismantling the argument of the Pharisees, or neatly discerning the thoughts of the woman at the well, or turning the water into wine at Cana, I admire him, but I tend to say, "I could never be like that." But when I encounter him in his agony, I start up in hope, saying, "Ahhh! He knows!"

But even in this prayer I find that I cannot be like Jesus. Always he sets forth the impossible model: "Be perfect, as your heavenly Father is perfect." And I don't have that in me. Maybe I can pray three times, "Let this cup pass," but I doubt I can say three times, "Thy will be done." Oh, of course I can *say* it, but can I *pray* it? That is, will I really mean it? Probably the first rule of prayer ought to be: let it be honest. God cannot be fooled. He knows whether I am really willing for his will to be done or not, so there is no use pretending to him. I can only fool myself into thinking I am pious when in fact I am simply scared to death. When someone we love has a deadly disease, or we are about to face a bad examination, or the cable-car feels like it's slipping, we'd better not pray, "Lord, thy will be done," unless we are extraordinary people. Better to pray, "Lord, *please* make him well!" "Lord, let me pass!" "Save me, Lord!" Better to pray, "Lord let our team win," in all honesty, than "May the best team win," in a pious attempt to impress God with our humility. He will not be fooled. He is the "Father who sees in secret" (Matt. 6:6) and knows what we need (Matt. 6:32). Better to be straight with him so that we will then be straight with ourselves.

## My God, my God, why hast thou forsaken me?

Matthew 27:46, Mark 15:34, Psalm 22:1

Thank God for that cry! To hear from Jesus' own lips an expression of his doubt and anxiety is to affirm him forever relevant to us ordinary mortals, and a source of our hope. As long as he appears as a super-hero, incapable of injury, something separates us. Try as I may, though he stands on the bank and offers his hand I cannot touch it, for I am unworthy. But when it suddenly dawns on me that he too is vulnerable, then my own vulnerability becomes bearable. So for this prayer of Jesus, as for his request in the garden for the cup's removal, again I give thanks.

For those among us who are shy of prayer books because they seem formal and rigid, note that here in his last hour Jesus was quoting from his prayer book, the book of Psalms. (Read Psalm 22. Doesn't it sound as though the Psalmist were a witness to the actual crucifixion?) This is the proper use of a traditional prayer. It has become such a part of our Lord, through his faithful devotions, that, in his agony he spills it forth. I remember a minister telling me that he had many times glibly read Psalm 130, "Out of the depths I cry to thee, O LORD," but it was not until his son was arrested one night for possession of narcotics that he suddenly found himself crying that verse as though it were really real.

In such a time, "My God!" is not an oath, it is a prayer. You may remember the tale about the pious actor who refused to say the line, "My God! I've been shot?" but substituted a euphemism such as "Good Heavens!" On the night of the performance, somebody put ketchup in the gun, and when he looked down at his bleeding chest, he cried, "My God! I *am* shot!"

A still more appropriate illustration is this line from George Macdonald:

> "O God!" I cried, and that was all. But what are the prayers of the whole universe more than expansions of that one cry? It is not what God can give us, but God that we want.*

---

*C. S. Lewis, *George Macdonald: An Anthology.*

96

*Father, into thy hands I commit my spirit.*

Luke 23:46, Psalm 31:5

If there was any doubt that Jesus' cry of agony was a quote from his prayer book, this act of surrender removes it. For it, too, is from the Psalms. Psalm 31 is a prayer of courage and hope in the face of great adversity, both of body and spirit. In such times, the Psalmist needs to reaffirm his trust. It is not that he must persuade God to remain faithful, rather, his own faith needs shoring up. Prayers in the last analysis are always addressed to a need in myself. In one sense they are the purest form of introspection. In this case, it is as though Jesus' answered his own cry, "God, where are you?" by reminding himself of the words of the Psalm:

> Be strong, and let your heart take courage,
> All you who wait for the LORD! (31:24)

Most of the time I am a phlegmatic person, who does not easily panic, but when things take me by surprise I sometimes go all to pieces. (I remember the time the flaming gasoline spilled on the straw tick in the fishing shack I was in, and how I carried away the four-by-four railing, 30-penny nails and all, and ended up in the lake.) For that reason I hope when I die I have some warning to get ready. I'd like time to remember Jesus' last words, for they would help me. Medical people tell me that when folk die, no matter how much struggling they do, eventually there comes a time when they surrender to death with a kind of calm. This could be interpreted in two ways. Either it is the surrender of ultimate despair . . . giving in to the inevitable, or it is the surrender of ultimate trust . . . coming home at last. We are free to make it what we will, but Jesus' example enables us to see it as victory, rather than defeat.

If there is any doubt about that, it is dispelled by John's account, in which Jesus says, "It is finished." It is an *Amen,* at the end of a short, tragic life, which changed the shape of the universe.

*Father, forgive them; for they know not what they do.*
Luke 23:34

This is the prayer that I don't understand. I can understand how he might feel forsaken by God. I can understand how he could come in the end to commitment and trust. I can understand how his own spiritual journey could reach its climax, even in the excruciating agony of crucifixion. But I don't understand how he could be thinking of others. What makes Jesus incredible is this continual self-emptying. How did he keep on giving and giving and giving, and still maintain his own integrity? Was he simply following supremely his own teaching: "He who loses his life . . . will find it"? (Matt. 10:39) Apparently his giving up of himself made him remember not only his friends (John 19:25–27), but a total stranger (Luke 23:39–43) and in this case, his executioners. He is like me when he cries out his doubts, but when he forgives his enemies, he is as different from me as God from humanity, east from west. Only divinity can forgive.

But it was for this cause that he came into the world, and he never forgot it. I used to have a secretary who always cursed under her breath whenever the phone rang: "O grumble that grumble grumble phone again. I never can get any of my work done without that grumble phone ringing." I never could get her to see that it was that grumble phone that made her job possible. She was *hired* to answer the telephone. Lawyers berate criminals, doctors denounce disease, and ministers preach against sin, but if it were not for them we'd be out of jobs.

If only my secretary could learn to say, "Oh boy, a ministry!" every time the phone rang, or I could learn to thank God for committee meetings as another chance to practice my compassion and share the gospel, then maybe we could learn to be like the Lord, who saw in his own ugly execution, another opportunity for mission. Or, to be more precise, who saw in his execution the supreme opportunity for ministry:

> I, when I am lifted up from the earth, will draw all men to myself.
> (John 12:32, see also 3:14; 8:28)

# I thirst.

John 19:28, (cf. Psalm 42:1–2)

When I first looked at the "Seven Last Words"* of Jesus, I thought that three of them, which begin by addressing God, were obviously prayers, while the other four, addressed to the persons around him (the thief, John, Mary, and his executioners) were not. But I find that won't do. For one thing, prayers to God are sometimes spoken to other persons: "God bless you," for example, really means, "I am praying to God that he will bless you." And for another, it isn't exactly clear who is the addressee of "I thirst," or "It is finished." Is he speaking these words to God, to the assembly, to himself, or just to the world? I have caught myself speaking aloud sometimes to no one in particular . For example, I remember having a flat tire, and while I was driving on the spare to a filling station, having another one. "Well, that does it," I said to the universe. (At any rate, that is the gist of what I said.) To whom is Jesus saying, "I thirst"?

John writes that he says it "to fulfill the scripture." But does John mean that Jesus deliberately tried to trick his captors into giving him vinegar, so that Psalm 69:21 would come true? I think not. Rather, what happened was that Jesus cried out because of a very real thirst, with the result that the scripture was fulfilled. In any event, this verse, like the "My God, why?" serves to reaffirm Jesus' humanity and make real his suffering. The Apostles' Creed has in it the line, "He descended into Hell." Whatever that means, it at least tells us that Jesus suffered total torment, both body and soul. "I thirst!" is his body's cry of pain; "My God!" is his soul's cry. They are the two basic prayers. If, in the Lord's Prayer, Jesus sanctions our asking for bread, surely by this, and by his own example, he makes it all right for us to pray for water. We must be careful to remember however, that in Jesus' case, the answer which came was not water but vinegar. That will enable us not to take our own droughts too seriously.

---

*The Seven Last Words are the last sentences spoken by Jesus from the cross as recorded in the four Gospels.

# VIII.
## BUILDING A PRAYER

*First of all, then, I urge that supplications, prayers, intercessions, and thanksgivings be made for all men, for kings and all who are in high positions, that we may lead a quiet and peaceable life, godly and respectful in every way.*

1 Timothy, 2:1–2

*Love your enemies and pray for those who persecute you.*

Matthew 5:44

*Pray that you may not enter into temptation.*

Matthew 26:41

*Is any one among you suffering? Let him pray. Is any cheerful? Let him sing praise. Is any among you sick? Let him call for the elders of the church, and let them pray over him, anointing him with oil in the name of the Lord; and the prayer of faith will save the sick man, and the Lord will raise him up; and if he has committed sins, he will be forgiven. Therefore confess your sins to one another, and pray for one another, that you may be healed. The prayer of a righteous man has great power. . . .*

James 5:13–16

# A MODEL FOR A GENERAL PRAYER

If you have been asked to offer a prayer before a group, or are searching for a formula for your own private prayers, this outline might help. (Of course, if you are by yourself, you will want to change the pronouns to "I.") This model doesn't pretend to be an ideal form for a general prayer, but an example to get you started. Your own heartfelt words will be best. See the following pages for examples to fill in the blanks.

| | |
|---|---|
| Address: | *Almighty God: (or other form)* |
| Qualifying phrase: | *(Something about God)* |
| Adoration: | *We praise you for* _____ |
| Confession: | *We admit that* _____ |
| Thanksgiving: | *We thank you that* _____ |
| Supplication: | *We need your help because (a need of your own)* ___ |
| Intercession: | *We pray for (the needs of others)* _____ |
| Closing formula: | *We make this prayer in Jesus' name.* |

It is not, of course, necessary to address God at all. A prayer can begin, and many do, as one resumes conversation with a person he knows well. But what we call God colors our understanding of him. And if we fall into the habit of repeating a standard formula for speaking to him, it ought to be a good one. At best, our terminology fails to pin him down. Even if we list all the words we can think of that tell what we believe about God (such as: "infinite, eternal, unchangeable in his being, wisdom, power, holiness, justice, goodness, and truth") that will not have described God. Anthony Bloom wrote:

> If we try and place ourselves before an image of God made up of all that we know of him through revelation, through the experience of the church, our own experience, we are in danger of standing before a false image, because it pretends to be a total image, when it can only ever be a poor approximation.*

So to escape this idolatry it is important that our concept of God continue to grow, to be sharpened, never become static. Here then, for use in training your mind on the eternal, are some ways of addressing the deity. Of course, neither does *this* list pretend to be other than idolatrous, but it is a place to start. You might pick out the form of address that suits you best and try using it for a time (a week, a month) and then use another one for a while.

*1. Names*
    a. *God.* Spelled with a capital G this is a proper name for the one object of supreme adoration; the Creator and Ruler of the universe. In the Old Testament it is the word usually used to translate the Hebrew word *El.* Strangely, this word is often found in its plural form, *Elohim,* but it usually is used in a singular sense, in what has been called "the plural of majesty," meaning that the Hebrew God is not one deity among many, but God of gods, or the One containing all lesser deities within himself.
    b. *Lord.* This is not, strictly speaking, a name for God but a title. But I have placed it here for an important (though a somewhat complicated) reason. In the Old Testament, God is called *Yahweh,* or perhaps *JHWH* (ancient Hebrew had no vowels). This divine name was not to be pronounced aloud by a mortal, so orthodox Hebrews substituted for it the title *Lord* (Hebrew, *Adonai*). The name *Jehovah* came into being, much later when vowels were added to the Hebrew. At that time, the vowels for the Hebrew word for the *Lord* were added to the consonants *JHVH.* In most of our English editions of the Bible, *JHVH* is

*Courage to Pray* (Paramus, N.J.: Paulist Press), p. 22.

translated *The LORD,* so that it has become almost equivalent to a name for him. (See page 44, as well as the discussion of *Lord* under "Titles," below.)

c. *Jesus.* Usually when I pray I begin with "God," or "Father," and at the end of the prayer add the formula "through Jesus Christ our Lord." I mean by that last that I am praying in the name and with the help of the One who is God's revelation as a historical human being. But some people accomplish the same thing by calling God *Jesus* when they pray. There are certainly good grounds for this (see for instance John 14:8–11). But to be technically correct (though no prayer should ultimately be judged on technicalities) we need to specify which Jesus we have in mind. The New Testament quite often gets very specific., e.g. Acts 4:10: "Jesus Christ of Nazareth." The name *Jesus* means in Hebrew "God is Salvation" and since the spelling of that ancient language has so many options we don't notice that there are a lot of familiar Bible people with that same name. *Joshua, Isaiah, Hosea,* and *Elisha* all mean "God is Salvation." (My favorite name is *Elijah,* which simply means, "God is Lord," that is, "El is JHWH.")

If you want to do a thorough study of the various ways of talking about or addressing Jesus, there is a very useful book by Vincent Taylor, called *The Names of Jesus,** which you should consult. Among others he lists the following:

Son of Joseph
Son of Mary
Teacher (Hebrew: *Rabbi*)
Prophet
Christ (Hebrew *Messiah,* the "anointed one")
Son of David
Son of Man (Jesus' own favorite way of referring to himself)
Son of God
King
Holy One
The One Who Comes
Righteous One
Judge
Lamb
Mediator
Bread of Life
Word
Power
Wisdom
Alpha and Omega (the first and last letters of the Greek alphabet)
Beloved

*London: Macmillan, 1953.

To this list we may add *Redeemer* (the only significant name for Jesus which originated outside of the Bible.)

d. *Holy Spirit.* This is what we usually call the third person of the Trinity. But it isn't really a name, it is a description. *Spirit* describes the nature of his existence; *Holy* describes his morality. He is an ethical God who "has not a body like man," and he is not to be confused with evil spirits. Not every voice that speaks to you in the night is the voice of God. It may even be something you ate or drank! For that reason it is hard to form a clear picture in the mind when saying the word *Spirit.* But some people use it because they dislike anthropomorphic pictures of God with a beard, like a Michelangelo painting. Go ahead, if that is where you are, but be careful that in throwing out the superstitious elements you are not simply substituting a "nothing," a God who, having no ears, cannot hear, and having no heart, cannot love. Possibly the next sections will help sharpen this for you.

## 2. Titles

It helps to qualify God's name with descriptive titles, precisely to avoid the vagueness mentioned in the last paragraph. The Bible is filled with them, and they are found in abundance in the great prayers of history. Here are a few:

a. *Lord* we have already mentioned; it is almost a name in many minds. But really it is an ancient title. In its Old English origins it meant "the head of a household," with authority over children and servants. As a translation of the Latin *dominus* and the Greek *kurios* it means one who has dominion or authority over others. When we call God *Lord* it implies our willingness to be obedient to him. There are other familiar titles, common in prayer, which are from the same general family of names, used to describe one to whom loyalty is owed: *King, Sovereign, Governor, Master.*

b. *Father* is Jesus' favorite title for God (which must say something about his own childhood under Joseph), and is the best word for God I know (which says something about my own childhood). But there are those for whom the word *father* conjures up an image of brutality, slovenliness, alcoholism, or even nonexistence. For them, perhaps, another term would be better. Carl Burke, in *God Is for Real, Man,** reports that some of the youngsters in the Buffalo jail preferred to liken God to a probation officer (which says something about the quality of the juvenile program in Erie County, N.Y.). Why not *Mother?* (See page 86)

c. *Shepherd* is a favorite, largely because of Psalm 23. But for many Americans, who live in urban areas and have never seen sheep being herded, it may lose some effectiveness. What would you substitute, given your cultural and geographical background, in finishing the sentence, "The Lord is like _____"?

d. Other titles you might use: Author, Judge, Guide, Rock, Might, Abyss,

*N.Y.: Association Press, 1966, p. 39.

Fountain, Sea (of goodness, etc.), Love, Brightness, Shield, Anchor, Hope, Consolation, Comfort, Foundation, Refuge, Strength, Peace, Life, Way, Truth, Light, Friend. You might try practicing with each of these in turn, in your prayers, and see what effect, if any, it creates.

### 3. Verbal Names

These too are titles, and sometimes more helpful, in that they enable us to address God at the same time we are keeping in mind one or more of his actions. This keeps us from falling into the trap of thinking of God as some kind of impersonal, formless something, but helps us to see him as the Bible sees him, One who acts in and through history, and in the lives of individuals:

Creator, Maker, Enlightener, Lover (of my soul, etc.), Comforter, Giver (of every good and perfect gift, etc.), Keeper, Defender, Redeemer, Savior, Restorer, Rescuer, Sanctifier, Helper, Bearer (of cares, etc.), Persuader, Ruler, Protector, Renewer.

You will have many more of your own which you will like better. (I privately think that if you are in doubt about a name for God, it will help you be on safe ground to use one from the Bible. But check the context in which it is used.)

### 4. Adjectives

Almighty, Holy, Heavenly, One, Living, Great, Omnipotent, Wise, Powerful, Just, Good, True, Merciful, Gracious, Glorious, Infinite, Eternal, Unchangeable, Sweet, Loving, Tender, Dear, Glorious, Unspeakable, Awful (full of awe), Immortal, Invisible, Wise, Sovereign, Blessed, Most High, First and Last, Ancient (of Days), etc.

To these are often added such qualifiers as: Most, All, Only, etc.

### 5. Qualifying Phrases

These sometimes begin with a relative pronoun, followed by a descriptive adjective:

"who art eternal" (since that involves the archaic form of the verb to be, *art,* you may want to say simply, "O God, you are eternal . . .")
or by a noun, as in:
Lord of: grace, compassion, love, power, wisdom, glory, our fathers, patience, consolation, hosts, etc.
or by a verb, or action phrase:
O God who acts, can, dost, never, knowest
or a prepositional phrase:
unto whom (all hearts are open, all desires known),
from whom (cometh every good and perfect gift).

There are limitless ways in which these phrases can be built to help us sharpen our image of the one to whom we are praying. It will not change him at all, but it will change us, as we grind out our faith against the Stone of Reality to whom we call.

## 6. Vocative Interjections

One word, finally, about those little cries that we sometimes utter at the beginning of a prayer: *O, Oh,* or *Ah,* etc. Sometimes we say, "O God," or sometimes simply, "O Thou," or even just "O." This is a deep primal sigh, from the heart, which you may feel like saying, or not. But if you are not in the habit of doing this, you might want to try it, in the privacy of your room or auto, and see what happens. Some of the mystics tell us that they have high experiences simply by saying over and over a simple phrase such as "O Lord . . . O Lord . . . O Lord . . ." until they begin to feel in tune with the infinite. From some of the Eastern cults has come the practice of saying the *Om,* that is, one long communal sigh, or groan, or hum, which the congregation may say together for many minutes until ecstatic prayers begin to happen. I can't advise you very much on this, but I know that you needn't be afraid to try, especially if you keep fast hold on your understanding of God as Jesus has shown him to us.

# THE ELEMENTS OF PRAYER

No prayer can contain everything; not every prayer needs to have all of these elements in it; though many do. This is merely a checklist which will be useful for you to run over when you prepare a prayer, to make sure that you are covering the whole range of possibilities. If you are called upon to pray in public this could be a guide for covering the needs of the congregation whom you are leading. Some people use the word ACTS as a mnemonic device for recalling the various elements: Adoration, Confession, Thanksgiving, Supplication and Intercession

I give them here just as they are found in the "Directory for the Worship and Work of the Church" found in *The Book of Church Order* of the Presbyterian Church in the United States, 1975.

"In *Adoration* the people are to adore the glory and perfection of God as they are made known in his works of creation and providence, in the clear and full revelation he has made in Jesus Christ, and in the work of the Holy Spirit."

"In *Thanksgiving* the people are to offer gratitude and praise to God for all his mercies, general and particular, spiritual and temporal; above all, for Christ Jesus, Savior and Lord, and for the life eternal which is in him."

(Frankly I don't see much difference between this and Adoration, except that it usually tends to be a little more personal.)

"In *Confession* the people are humbly to acknowledge unto God their sinfulness in nature and in act, and their sins both of omission and commission, with a deep sense of the evil of all sin committed against God, our neighbor, and ourselves. They shall ask forgiveness through Jesus Christ. The confession should be concluded by the Minister's affirming the assurance of pardon through Jesus Christ as promised in Holy Scripture."

I go along with that, except that I don't see why a "minister" has to announce that pardon. It has already been declared in Scripture, and anyone can deliver the message, if they know about it. Some great passages of Scripture that make good Declarations of Pardon are John 3:16; 2 Cor. 5:19; 1 John 4:10; Psalm 103:8–13; Psalm 32; Isaiah 6; 1 John 1:8–9. This announcement can also precede the confession; perhaps it always should. God's forgiveness is not dependent upon the effectiveness of our praying; it happened long ago on Calvary. What hangs in the balance is our acceptance of it, as his gift. In earthly relationships we rarely confess our sin to those whom we do not trust, and from whom we have not been given in advance at least some indication that they will not reject us when we tell them the truth about ourselves. So God, making himself known in Christ, opens the door for our confession. His pardon both precedes and follows our prayer. The good news of the gospel is always appropriate.

"In *Supplication* the people are to ask earnestly through Jesus Christ for the outpouring of the Holy Spirit, for peace with God accompanied by all the fruits of that peace, for abundant supplies of the grace necessary to enable them to be obedient unto God, for support and comfort under trials, and for needed temporal blessings."

Indeed, we might add that Jesus encourages us to ask for whatever we will (Matt. 7:7–11). He promises that if we ask for bread, he will not give us a stone. Not even an earthly father, mean as we are, would do that. And if we stupidly ask for a stone to eat, it follows that our Heavenly Father would answer that prayer, not by giving us what we said we wanted, but what we really wanted: namely bread.

"In *Intercession* the people are to offer petition on behalf of others: for the visible kingdom of Christ, his Church Universal; for the interest and welfare of human society; and for all to whom God has given civil authority."

It is pretty important that such prayers be specific, to keep us from lapsing into vague generalities which will not alter our lives, but only make us think we have been religious. Here is a checklist of matters that a general intercession might include:

> the whole earth, particularly trouble spots
> the church throughout the world
> the church in this place (where the prayer is offered)
> peace
> our enemies
> national and local officials (These, including presidents and kings should be
>     referred to by first names, [e.g. Jimmy, our President] to remind ourselves
>     that nobody has any special status before God. Or rather, that we all have
>     great status!)
> world leaders and the United Nations
> daily work
> the sick (it would be good to remember them by name)
> world hunger
> the bereaved
> those far from home
> the communion of saints (I love that great old phrase. It is really a prayer
>     for the ultimate reunion of all God's people, past, present, and future. It
>     gives us a chance to remember our mothers and fathers who have died,
>     and to give a fresh chance for grieving to those who are bereaved.)

# IX.
## SOME NECESSARY MECHANICS

*I desire then that in every place the men should pray, lifting holy hands.*

1 Timothy 2:8

*And he came out, and went, as was his custom, to the Mount of Olives; and the disciples followed him. And when he came to the place he said to them, "Pray that you may not enter into temptation." And he withdrew from them about a stone's throw, and knelt down and prayed.*

Luke 22:39–41

*And going a little farther, he fell on the ground and prayed.*

Mark 14:35

*And he entered the temple and began to drive out those who sold, saying to them, "It is written, 'My house shall be a house of prayer'; but you have made it a den of robbers."*

Luke 19:45–46

# POSTURE IN PRAYER

The Presbyterian Directory says, "The posture of the people in public prayer should always be reverent." That frees them from having to kneel like Episcopalians, and warns them against rolling about like Pentecostals. But, unfortunately, it doesn't offer much guidance. My own idea is that whatever posture is your habit, you probably ought to try another one. If you never kneel, doing so might give your mind some signals that would really help you to see things in a different way. If you have always knelt, consider the counsel given me by a Catholic priest, who pointed out that kneeling originated in an era when this was the way one greeted a Lord, political or religious. "But today," he said, "what do you do when the king or the president enters the room? You stand!" Thus he suggests standing as an attitude of reverence.

You might even want to go further than that and use your body in specially dramatic gestures. Children and ballet artists will know what I mean here. If you are interested, I suggest you read *Congregational Dancing in Christian Worship*, by Doug Adams, available from The Enabling Company, (1972), 1035 Indiana St., Vallejo, California. This interesting book contains, among other things, some simple suggestions for using hand gestures or bodily movements to The Lord's Prayer and others. If you have some professional dance people in your church, they can help. There is a motion picture called *The Dancing Prophet* (produced by Franciscan Communications Center, 1229 S. Santee St., Los Angeles, CA 90015; phone: 213–748–2191) which would be helpful here; the film is available from the producer and some religious libraries.

You don't need to shut your eyes. It might even help to look at some object while you pray. Or into the face of a friend. Or in the mirror.

But the important thing is, do it! Forget how you stand, let your hands and arms do what they feel like doing.

Read Luke 18:13–14.

# WHERE AND WHEN TO PRAY

Anywhere, anytime, all the time.

I read somewhere about a man whose whole life-style was changed while waiting for a traffic signal. He was grumbling to himself at the delay, the way he usually did, when it suddenly dawned on him: "What a wonderful thing it is to live in a world in which half of the population will agree to wait while the other half goes!" This concept restored his faith in the human race. Now, he says, he uses his moments of waiting at the stop-light to think creative and positive thoughts. His discovery prompted me to make use of life's little delays as prayer time. (When I first began to think of this book I had the idea of printing it with long narrow pages so that the book would fit on the dash-board of a car. It would be called "Prayers to Be Prayed While Waiting for the Traffic Light to Change." But I decided the National Safety Council wouldn't approve.)

This appeals to me because I have never been very good at regularly scheduled devotions. Something is always interrupting prayers at meals, bedtime, or morning. (It is often my laziness, procrastination, or general unwillingness to sit under the discipline of an ordered devotional life.) Frankly I'm sorry about that, and I cordially recommend that you develop such a regular plan for praying. But just because you haven't yet become a perpetual pray-er, don't let that stop you from praying every chance you get.

Sometimes, in restaurants or other public places, I do my praying secretly; that is, not to make a big thing out of bowing and shutting my eyes. That way, I don't embarass the people around me who haven't learned to accept prayer as a natural part of life. Sometimes it may be good to do it overtly (because some people need to be embarassed, or shocked, or evangelized) but be careful that you know why you are doing this. Be very sure it is not simply to impress them with your piety. We are forbidden from this (Matt. 6:1–8). If you insist on doing it anyway, prepare to suffer the consequences of being misunderstood.

Many of us have become accustomed to having all public prayer reduced to one method: a leader (usually a paid professional) stands before the group and prays at them. This is by no means the only way. Indeed, it can be very destructive. Kierkegaard wrote long ago:

> ... the speaker is not the actor—not in the remotest sense. No, the speaker is the prompter. There are no mere theatergoers present, for each listener will be looking into his own heart. The stage is eternity .... God is the critical theatergoer. ... The listener, if I may say so, is the actor, who in all truth acts before God.*

There are lots of ways of doing it which do not lock us into the lecture-listen, or performer-audience mode. If you are a worship leader, or get called upon to lead in public prayer, you may want to run down this list and use it as a starter for thinking how you would get the congregation involved in the praying with you.

1. Use prayers written by members of the group.

2. Get a group together beforehand to plan the praying, so that it isn't just your ideas.

3. Have the congregation compose the prayer on the spot by calling out in a word or phrase those things for which they would like to give thanks, or confess, or ask for help.

4. After such one-word prayers the people can make them their own by saying or singing responses:

Leader: Praise the Lord!

People: The Lord's Name Be Praised!

or

Leader: Hear our prayer, Lord!

People: And let our cry come unto you!

5. Be silent, for a long time, and let people make their own private prayers. This may eventually produce some spontaneous praying by the congregation.

6. Use unison prayers which have become established in the church's tradition, either in official prayer books, or other collections.

7. Use prayers out of the Bible. (E.g. Psalm 51, and others quoted in this book.)

8. Alternate Confession and Praise, and change the response from *Praise the Lord!* to the *Kyrie*. A note about that venerable versicle! The words *Kyrie Eleison*

---

*Purity of Heart Is to Will One Thing*, Trans. by Douglas V. Steere (N.Y.: Harper & Brothers, 1938), pp. 163–164.

are Greek, and they are, oddly enough, the opening words of the Latin Mass! They were so familiar to worshipers that when the service was first translated from Greek into Latin (that Vulgar tongue!) it just didn't sound like church without the *Kyrie* at the beginning, so they left it in. (It must have been even harder to get from Hebrew into Greek, because God speaks Hebrew, as we all know.) It can be sung penitentially:

Lord have mercy upon us!

or triumphantly:

You are the Lord, giver of mercy!

There are lots of good tunes that it can be done to. See *The Worshipbook*, especially the folk setting, page 253.

9. Have people make sentence prayers. (Watch out that this doesn't degenerate into a brag session, particularly if it is to be confession.)

10. "Prayers in pairs." Let people, if they don't feel like speaking out before the large group, share their concerns with the persons next to them.

11. Have a bidding prayer. This is one in which the leader names several subjects, like the list on page 109, and the people pray silently.

12. Use the daily newspaper as a source of matters for prayer. The headlines alone can be an effective starter.

13. Use a litany. (See *The Worshipbook*, pages 103–131.)

14. Compose your own litany. This can be done on the spot, without even a mimeograph machine, simply by asking the people to respond with a phrase, such as, "Hear our prayer, O Lord," or, "Help us, good Lord." It is perfectly OK to stop in the middle and change the response.

15. Have a photographer in your congregation take slides to illustrate your litany and let the people look at them as they pray, as visual aids to prayer.

16. Encourage the people to take part in the prayers by saying the *Amen.* If necessary, at first, you can give them a cue phrase, such as "through Jesus Christ, our Lord," so they will know when to say it. Later, perhaps, they will come to feel all right about saying it at any time.

17. You might even try having everybody pray out loud at once their own prayers. This is done in some far-Eastern churches and by Pentecostal groups in this country. It creates an interesting wave of sound throughout the congregation, coming to a stop on its own when everyone is through.

18. Of course, if it comes to it, you can always pray yourself, and let the others go along silently, in the traditional manner. If you do this, it will be to your advantage if you avoid pious phraseology, cute language, and Elizabethan English. Not that you shouldn't plan your prayers carefully, writing them out if you have time. I know that it seems that "reading" a prayer is stiff and formal, while praying extemporaneously feels more natural. But this is really an illusion. Nearly everybody who prays "off the cuff" follows an unconscious ritual which is just as fixed and formal as a written prayer. (You probably remember some preachers

in your childhood whose prayers were so unconsciously ritualistic that you could predict with accuracy how much longer they had to go.) And you don't have to "read" a written prayer. *Pray* it! That is, say those words with feeling, emotion, and reverence. If you meant them when you wrote them you can mean them just as much when you repeat them later. Only a very skilled pray-er can avoid the trap of the unconscious liturgy. Better to study and use great prayers, write out your own, struggle and work with them, and then, one day, when you are called upon by life or by some emergency to pray spontaneously, the words will come. (Matt. 10:19)

# HOW TO STOP PRAYING

Too much length is the fault of many public prayers, if not private ones. I remember once when a man, unaccustomed to public praying, was called upon to lead in prayer. Rather than admit his incompetence, he launched out. Actually he did rather well, but his mind drew a blank when he tried to recall the traditional closing formula, "through Jesus Christ our Lord." Frantically he prayed for every subject under heaven while he wracked his brain for a way out. At last (at long last) he cried in desperation, "Yours truly, Amen!" I laughed at the time, but in my declining years I have come to wonder if he hasn't hit on something.

The important thing is to say it and be done. Or else someone should (as they say D. L. Moody once did) interrupt and say, "While the good brother continues to talk to the Lord, the rest of us will sing Hymn No. 352." Most prayers can be short. When you do come to the end, remember that the *Amen* is not a part of the prayer. The prayer ends with the period after the last sentence, which may follow the phrase, "through Jesus Christ our Lord." The *Amen* means "me too," or "right on" or "let it be" and properly belongs to the rest of the assembly. If you are praying by yourself it is redundant. However, you may say it, if what you mean by it is something like this:

> *Well, Lord, I have done the best I know how, and I stand by it. I know it wasn't much, but it was all I knew. Yes I know I COULD have done better if I had worked harder, but I didn't and there's no use trying to cover up, so it will just have to stand as it is. May your grace turn it into something worth saying.*

Amen.

# X.
# SOME HELPFUL BOOKS

The Bible, of course, especially the Book of Psalms. Be sure to look at 1 Corinthians 11—14, Matthew 6, and John 14—17.

*The Book of Common Prayer* of the Episcopal Church is a must, no matter what your denomination.

*The Worshipbook* of the Presbyterian Church has an excellent collection of prayers on many subjects. (If you are neither a Presbyterian nor an Episcopalian, be sure to look at the service book of your own communion.)

*The Directory for Worship* or other official position paper of your denomination.

Baillie, John. *A Diary of Private Prayer.* New York: Scribner's, 1949. A modern classic, introducing us to the prayer life of an eminent pastor and scholar.

Bonhoeffer, Dietrich. *Psalms: The Prayer Book of the Bible.* Minneapolis: Augsburg, 1970. A little gem, introducing us to Jesus' use of the Psalms.

Buttrick, George A. *Prayer.* Nashville: Abingdon, 1942.The most thorough book ever written on the subject. Relevant and inspiring.

Fosdick, Harry Emerson. *A Book of Public Prayers.* New York: Harper, 1959. Some beautiful examples of a clergyman at work at the art of praying.

Head, David. *He Sent Leanness.* New York: Macmillan, 1959. A sad, lovely, ironic commentary on prayer in the church today by one who understands.

Law, William. *A Serious Call to a Devout and Holy Life.* New York: Dutton, 1972. The classic Puritan statement on a life of prayer and service.

Lewis, C. S., *Letters to Malcolm: Chiefly on Prayer.* New York: Harcourt Brace Jovanovich, 1964. A light, somewhat informal glimpse into this remarkable man's theory and practice of prayer.

Lewis, C. S., *Miracles: A Preliminary Study.* New York: Macmillan, 1963. A more formal treatise on the power of God to intervene in human life. (Particularly the last section on intercessory prayer.)

Micklem, Caryl, ed. *Contemporary Prayers for Public Worship.* Grand Rapids: Eerdmans, 1967. An effective attempt by some Episcopalians to make a fresh approach at their ancient liturgical skill.

Tileston, Mary Wilder, *Prayers, Ancient and Modern.* A collection of prayers, not too selective, but useful as a look at the possibilities.

White, James F. *New Forms of Worship.* Nashville: Abingdon, 1971. Perhaps the best current book on the biblical and historical basis for renewal in liturgical practice. Lucidly written.

Bash, Ewald, *Songs for Today.* A delightful collection, mainly of Psalms set to folk tunes, published by the Youth Department of the American Lutheran Church.